How to Get a

J-O-B

*An Eight-Step Program for
Lawyer Employment*

Nelson P. Miller

How to get a J-O-B: an eight-step program for lawyer employment.

Miller, Nelson P.

Published by:

Crown Management LLC – October 2016

1527 Pineridge Drive
Grand Haven, MI 49417
USA

ISBN: 978-0-9980601-2-5

*For job seekers who really **do** want to find a job.*

Summary Table of Contents

Detailed Table of Contents

Research Goal 28
Negative Research Results 28
Identify and Pursue Trends 29
Solo Practitioners 31
Specific Employer Information 31

Step 4: **Develop Your Resources** 33

Your Resources Matter 33
Your Resume 34
Resume Themes 35
Resume Types 35
Resume Details 36
Other Resume Sections 37
Multiple Resumes 38
Electronic Resumes 39
Electronic Resume Keywords 40
Your Cover Letter 41
Cover Letter Form and Contents 42
Your Writing Sample 43
Recommendation Letters 45
References 46
Professional Portfolios 47
Presenting Your Portfolio 48
Other Resources 49
Your Character and Skills Matter 50
Know Your Character and Skills 51
Discern Your Unique Qualities 52
Share Your Character and Skills 53
Show More than Tell 54

Step 5: **Build Your Network** 55

Why Networks Matter 55
Everyone Has a Network 56
List Network Contacts 56
Expand Your Network 57
Employ Your Network 58
Writing Thank-You Notes 59
Other Network Etiquette 60
Email Etiquette 61
A Recording System 62

Step 6: **Discover Job Openings** 64

Discovering Job Openings Matters 64

Introduction

You Need Both a Plan and Proof

A successful job search requires two things, (1) a sound plan and (2) the inspiration to implement it. This book gives both to law students and lawyers who are seeking a job. Part I is a deliberate, thoughtful, eight-step plan around which you can easily and continuously organize, implement, and assess your job search. Your job search needs sound structure. To find your desired job in a reasonable time while managing your transition and minimizing stress, you need to address comprehensively and consistently, and in coordinated fashion, any number of critical but discrete and elusive tasks. Part I offers you that plan in the form of an electronic journal that you will use to record, monitor, and assess your job search. Yet you also need energy, confidence, and inspiration to carry out your job search. You will find those necessary attributes most readily in proof that your job search will succeed. Part II gives you that proof in a collection of accounts of varied job-search successes. Part II titles each account uniquely to show you how fortuitous job searching can be. You need to be deliberate, even plodding, which is Part I. You also need to trust the process enough to pursue it diligently, expecting surprising and satisfying results, which is Part II. Enjoy the book, and enjoy the job search.

1

Part I

Get with the Program

Your Program Matters

You are holding more than just another book on job searching. Here, you have a job-search *program*. Yes, you should find much helpful job-search information as you read this book. Yet you can find job-search information and advice everywhere. Those who are trying to land a job need more than information. You need action, *effective* action. You need to get off your proverbial duff to turn information, thoughts, and plans into results-oriented acts that carry you ever closer to a job. When the subject comes to job search, sitting is the new smoking. Just thinking without acting will be deadly to your job-search success. You need to act and not just act haphazardly but instead in just the right ways to lead to the job that will meet your career goals. Think of job *search* instead as job *development*. You almost have to *make* your job, *create* your job, or at least *coax* your job into fruition. Don't expect your job to come trotting happily up to you wagging its tail to get your attention — although with the right action that happy event happens, too. Embrace this book's *program* more than its *information*. If you think this section reads like a bit of a kick in the pants, then fine. One new lawyer who (much to his surprise) quickly found a great new job said that his gruff military-veteran

3

father gave him the best job-search advice: quit expecting anyone to hand anything to you. The job that you need is right there. Go get it.

Program Steps

The following chapters will lead you through the program's steps or components, each of which is really a job-search strategy. The chapter titles, order, and content make clear each of the steps and their purpose. The value of each step should quickly become obvious to you. Yet while the program's steps are orderly and progressive, you need not, indeed *should not*, work on only one step at a time in sequence. Rather, your key overarching strategy is to work wherever your inspiration, contacts, thoughts, actions, and experiences take you. Because the program's steps are all natural, necessary, and helpful, you will quickly find that you are working on all steps, even if not sequentially. Appreciate what you are accomplishing as you work on your job search in this inspired, flexible, but thoughtful fashion. Fundamentally, you realize and confirm things about yourself, some of which you may have long known but others of which may surprise and reward you. You also hone your ability to present and represent yourself in ways that benefit and attract others. You are also learning and perfecting important planning, implementation, and assessment skills that you will go on using for other purposes well beyond your job search. Finally, even as you search for your job, you should be establishing a foundation of understanding, confidence, and discernment that will help you integrate your job into a balanced and rewarding life.

Get Started—Now

So, to get started, simply open a new, blank word-processing file, title it *Job Search*, and save it electronically in your most prominent and accessible folder or other location. Put your *Job Search* file where you will encounter it frequently throughout your day and week as you use your electronic devices. Making it prominent and accessible will encourage you to use it more frequently and productively. There now. Pat yourself on the back. You have done the hardest part already, which is to take the first intentional step in your job search. Every next step will make you feel more and more like you are running downhill toward your job. Next, in the minute or two that it will take you, type this program's ten chapter titles into your *Job Search* file as follows: **Step 1** Confirm My Commitments; **Step 2** Analyze My Skills; **Step 3** Evaluate My Market; **Step 4** Develop My Resources; **Step 5** Discover My Opportunities; **Step 6** Confirm My Network; **Step 7** Apply, Apply, Apply; and **Step 8** Manage My Transition. Congratulations. You are now ready for action.

Write It Down

Your simple task in this program is to record in your *Job Search* file **everything** that you do connected in any way with your job search. This program works from the well-known principle that *what gets recorded gets attention*. The more that you reflect on and record your job-search actions, the more attention you will likely give them. Your key is to make entries in your *Job Search* file for any of its ten steps at once, back and forth, wherever your insights, contacts, and efforts take you daily. Work on every step at once, or focus on any one for a time, but no matter what, keep recording what you think and do in your job search. Review your *Job Search* file daily, preferably at a routine time to ensure its consistent review, to ensure that you capture every small or large job-search insight or activity that you had that day and that you know what you need to do going forward. Creating, maintaining, and expanding your *Job Search* file enables you to see at a glance how much you have done in your job search. Reflecting and recording will make you want to do more job searching. Success in anything requires planning, preparation, and persistent implementation and assessment. Expect your *Job Search* file to expand quickly to five pages, ten pages, and even as many as twenty to thirty pages long before you get your first solid job offer. Have at it. Get to it. Write it down. Review it. Keep at it.

Evaluate and Revise

As you review your *Job Search* file daily, evaluate and revise your prior entries. Rather than delete prior entries that proved unhelpful, use strikethrough font ~~like this~~ so that you can still read what you revised or corrected. Use red highlighting (indicating to *stop* and *avoid*) for activities that you tried but that did not work, although do not be hasty in making this judgment. Perseverance can pay off when early indications do not look promising. Just because one person or employer discourages you from an activity or practice does not mean that others will also fail to appreciate it. Use green highlighting (indicating *go* and *repeat*) for activities that prove useful. Highlight in yellow (indicating *alert* and *pay attention*) what you need to do next. Doing so will decrease unfruitful activities while increasing fruitful activities, all by enabling you to see at a glance what is either working or not working, and what needs attention. Aside from planning, recording, and assessing your job-search activities, also use this record to develop your job-search knowledge and resources, through Steps 3 and 4. At night and on weekends, or at other odd times when you cannot be pounding the proverbial pavement, work on Steps 3 and 4. If you get discouraged, then work on Step 8, having to do with managing your transition into the job, choosing the job, and starting the job right.

Career Skills

Even as you search for a job, value what you learn in doing so. The skills that you learn and confirm from your job search will very likely not be skills that you use once and then ignore for a lifetime. New employees entering the workforce in this twenty-first century are very likely to change jobs frequently. The days of the twenty- to forty-year career are for the most part long gone. New employees changing jobs every two to three years may be closer to the norm than the aberration. Many new employees may have as many as ten or more different jobs in their first twenty working years. Many of those job moves may be by choice, as new employees seek better work for better pay. Other job moves will not be by choice, as new employees find employer needs changing swiftly in a global economy that reacts swiftly to technological, financial, political, social, and other change. New employees, mid-career employees, and employees close to retirement all may find job-search skills necessary at a moment's notice or helpful from time to time. Professionals today should think of job-search skills not as something that only recent college or professional-school graduates need but rather career-long skills.

Time Management

Whether you believe it or not, you have the time. I know, I know: you are *very* busy. We are all busy, busier than we should be. New lawyers are especially busy graduating, moving, preparing for bar exams and licensure, and often marrying, having children, and working in old or new but temporary jobs while they look for that first big law job. Mid-career and senior lawyers are also very busy with their current employers, practices, clients, and commitments, feeling barely able if able at all to look for that next, better job. Who isn't busy these days? Yet the job-search activities that this program requires are not big-chunk time sinks. Rather, they are better done in frequent small time increments. You can accomplish a lot with a little (time), as long as you act often, promptly, swiftly, wisely, and efficiently. Two minutes here, five minutes there, twenty minutes there again, all add up. Studies of lawyers and law students find that while nearly all of us are very good at organizing and prioritizing, we are often not very good at present orientation. When we have five minutes to do one quick job-search task, we will often instead simply ruminate and regret about not having the time to do it.

Instead, maintain the attitude to *git 'er done*, right now. You have the time if you just commit to using it frequently and promptly.

Passion

So, before you begin, let's consider once again the theme of *getting with the program*. The days of employers begging you to work for them are long over, if indeed those days ever existed, which they largely didn't. You must truly *want* to get a job before you *will* get a job. You have to be hungry, craving, starving, and passionate, not crazed or desperate, but genuinely earnest to the point of ardent pursuit. If you don't yet have that feeling, then examine yourself closely. *You* are your biggest obstacle, not the employment market, or the economy, or your lower class standing at graduation, or even your inexpensive suit and haircut (although it might not hurt to attend a little more to your first appearance). Clear your mind and attitude of all the justifications for maybe why you *don't* want a job just yet. Stop telling yourself that living in your parents' basement isn't all that bad, or you can wait a few more years to get married, or just maybe you were borne to be a surfer or Sufi rather than a lawyer. Clear your mind and attitude of the external, uncontrollable influences over your job prospects, like whether a certain firm or agency is hiring right now, so that you can focus on the internal and personal things that you *can* control. Get out of your own way long enough to get moving and *keep* moving until you have coaxed that job out of the proverbial woods. Your job is there for you. You just have to go get it, and not willy-nilly but thoughtfully, with a set of clear and coordinated actions like those that you had to follow to earn your law degree. You can do it. Many have done it before you, and many will do it after you. You can do it.

STEP 1:

Confirm Your Commitments

Your Commitments Matter

Your *Job Search* file, the one that you already opened in your word-processing program and gave that title, begins with **Step 1** to *Confirm Your Commitments.* What does confirming commitments mean, and why would you begin a job search by doing so? Each of us has certain principles, relationships, causes, and commitments that we value. We hold those commitments above other things. Take the example of *providing for myself* or even *providing for my family.* Rightly or wrongly, fairly or unfairly, and for better or worse, some of us just aren't that concerned about earning our own keep, while others of us make doing so our number one priority. If that is you, that you more than anything else want the pride, satisfaction, and accountability of having provided for yourself and family members, then record that commitment under **Step 1**. Let that commitment get you up early in the morning. Let it keep you working on job development late at night. On the other hand, for some of us, meaningful work doesn't mean putting food on the table but instead means following your passions, pursuing causes, experiences, and affinities. If that is you, that you care more about what you do than what doing something, *anything,* provides for you and family, then record that commitment under **Step 1**. Let that commitment get you up early. Let it keep you up late at night. The important thing is to list in **Step 1** your passions and commitments, things that get you excited and carry you through. List anything that will ensure that you do the right things with the right intentions reaching the right results of getting the right job consistent with your core commitments. You have permission to have ideals even when doing something as practical as searching for a job. Refer to your ideals and commitments whenever you question your integrity or the integrity of your job-search process.

Think Deeply and Broadly

Do not be surprised if you initially can hardly think of any commitments but if later you realize that you have many commitments. In other words, let this part of your job-search file develop over time. Don't force it. Let it percolate. Think of your desires in the broad arc of your life. Think, too, of your temperament, character, experiences, and attitudes. You may, for instance, realize that your number one commitment is not to the job or yourself but to the care, nurture, or other welfare of a spouse, parent, child, or significant other. That commitment to, say, a spouse's career interests or the stability of a child's relationships and home may mean that you must find a job in a certain location for at least a certain time. Recognize and record the commitment first. Know why you are pursuing what you think that you need to pursue. Push yourself to identify, say, a *dozen* things that you hope to uphold, confirm, respect, and accomplish, and then prioritize those things. Then recognize how that commitment establishes the parameters or goals for your job search. Keep exploring your commitments as they arise. Why, for instance, do you believe that you need a job that will enable you to work flexible hours (a suspected parameter or goal)? Record the commitment, perhaps to the special episodic care of an elderly parent or disabled child, underlying that parameter or goal. If you don't record the commitment and instead only record the parameters or goals, then you may miss something important.

11

You may unwittingly make commitments that you don't actually hold. Or vice versa, you may miss keeping commitments that you dearly hold. Record the commitments, not just the goals.

What Are Your Goals?

Notice again from the prior paragraph that commitments differ from goals. Commitments should lead to goals. Your next step, then, still here in **Step 1**, is to list the goals that you derive from your commitments. For example, if your number one commitment is to provide for yourself and your family, then your goal is pretty obviously to get a job. But what job or, more precisely, with what income that would actually further your commitment to provide? Indeed, a commitment to provide might lead you to any number of goals to get a job within a certain amount of time with a certain income and benefits including things like health insurance and retirement contributions. A commitment to do work that you enjoy might include goals to work with certain co-workers sharing your affinities and interests, or to work in a certain field, or to work with certain clients, or to work in a certain setting, whether office, clinic, court, agency, nonprofit, or so forth. A commitment to lead a balanced work life might lead to goals on hours, vacations, commute time and distance, and schedule flexibility. The point here is that your commitments should generate goals. Just thinking about how your commitments connect with certain goals can lead you to important revelations about your job search. List both long-term, broad life goals and shorter-term intermediate goals, the latter more measurable, timed, and specific. Listing commitments and goals may be far from anything practical for getting a job, but then again, you are not holding up any other step while you make notes about commitments and goals. You are instead pursuing all other steps even while you capture here under **Step 1** notes about goals and commitments. Indeed those **Step 1** notes may lead you directly to doing some highly practical work that gets you the job that is best for you.

Recognize Obstacles

As you list your long-term and short-term goals, you will likely perceive various obstacles to those goals. Don't hesitate to list and even analyze those obstacles in **Step 1**. Know thy enemy as well as thy friend. Law students, lawyers, and other professionals face many and varying obstacles. Health conditions and disabilities can present substantial challenges at various times and in various stages or settings. Indeed, very few of us go a lifetime without one or more serious health conditions or substantial disabilities, even if only of shorter rather than longer or permanent duration. Time may also be a specific obstacle particularly for professionals with children, other dependents, or other unusual obligations. Finances, credit history, and debt can become obstacles. A past character-and-fitness issue may be a particular obstacle in a job search. If you have a current character-or-fitness or other life-controlling issue, such as substance abuse, compulsive spending, or an abusive relationship, then recognize *and address* that obstacle with special commitment and diligence. Dealing in a job search with one's own checked past is a navigable challenge. Do not enter a job search bound by an ongoing issue when you have the power to correct, address, and end it. In your **Step 1** self-assessment, include not just commitments and goals, but weaknesses and obstacles that might prevent you from keeping commitments and attaining goals. Then deal with those weaknesses and obstacles to the full extent that you are able. Some law students overcome remarkable issues to become an outstanding lawyer. Much is possible, but only if you deal forthrightly with the obstacles. The point with goal setting is to be realistic. Recognize significant limitations so that you can plan to account for, address, avoid, or ameliorate them.

Clarify Values and Preferences

As you work through identifying your commitments and goals, also clarify your values and preferences. Law practice can be a powerful, indeed even intoxicating, experience. Lawyers need to be more intentional than some other professionals and employees in integrating their work into a healthy lifestyle. Any job can destroy your health and relationships. On the other hand, many jobs can also contribute mightily to your health and relationships. By identifying your values and preferences during your job search, you increase the chance that you will make wise decisions about which jobs for which to apply, which job to accept, what terms on which to accept it, and how to carry out the job while preserving your health and relationships. Lifestyle preferences, such as warm weather or seasonal climate, and country living or metropolitan living, are easy to identify. Don't hesitate to do so. While **Step 1** is primarily about deeper commitments, don't hesitate to record lifestyle preferences. Some of us draw significant and even priority commitments out of lifestyle preferences. Some lawyers value surfing as much as they do anything else. Yet beyond discerning obvious lifestyle preferences, clarifying your values can be harder. Try choosing and recording in **Step 1** your priority values from this alphabetical list, and then assembling them into a thematic value statement: adventure; advocacy; appearance; arts; collaboration; conflict; creativity; engagement; entertainment; faith; fame; family; healing; helping; honesty; honor; independence; influence; integrity; intellectual curiosity; learning; legacy; leisure; liberty; loyalty; management; morality; partnership; physical health and fitness; opportunity; order and organization; peace and comfort; power; prestige; productivity; respect; security; service; solitude; supervision; sustainability; teamwork; and wealth.

Know Your Personality

Your personality lies somewhere in this complex job-search mix of commitments, values, and preferences. Knowing your personality can help you make sound judgments about the jobs that you should and should not pursue, even though the judgments are not necessarily that easy or obvious. Don't refuse to pursue a job just because you think that you are an introvert

14

rather than an extrovert. Your personality may actually differ from what you think, and the work that a certain law job requires may also differ from what you think, in the personality types that it attracts. Yet the mantra remains that you benefit by knowing thyself. If you know that you tend strongly toward an introvert's personality, think logically before you feel emotionally, or prefer a planned and predictable environment over spontaneity, then that insight could well guide you somewhere along your job path. The contrasts just mentioned are from the Myers-Briggs Type Indicator® that you may well have taken in law school. Myers-Briggs is a popular instrument to help assess personality types. Use your Myers-Briggs results, or take it or another assessment, for insight into your personality and preferences. Some employers require employees or job candidates to complete personality or other similar assessments. You may as well know your own personality if your employer is also interested in discovering it. Record your personality type in **Step 1**, and refer to it from time to time for insight on your best job match. Workplaces vary widely in their environments and conditions. Lawyers, like other professionals, may work in an office or from home, on a fixed or flexible schedule, with constant or rare interpersonal interactions, under deadlines or at their own pace, with contingent or fixed income, alone or in teams, independently or under supervision, and under other varying conditions. Project how your personality may fit under those conditions.

STEP 2:

Analyze Your Skills

Your Skills Matter

Funny thing, but employers actually pursue skilled employees. The employment relationship is not entirely about you getting a paycheck, benefits, or a balanced and meaningful work life. It is also about you providing labor of value to your employer in return. To be effective at job searching, you should both know your skills *and* be able to communicate them clearly and effectively to interested employers. To communicate your skills, you could do no better than to start in **Step 2** by listing them. Your **Step 2** list may or may not translate into any new statements on your resume. The accomplishments that you list on your resume may alone imply certain skills. You don't have to adopt an explicitly skills-based resume format in order to communicate your skills. If you know your skills well, then your cover letter, introductory emails, brief elevator speech, interview, and other communications are likely to reflect your skills knowledge. You will naturally communicate your skills if you have first been intentional about identifying them. If you cannot make a decent list on your own, then ask your family, friends, co-workers, and former employers. They may know more about your skills than you know yourself. Let your law school's career coordinator help you generate an accurate list reflecting your own

16

skills from the coordinator's knowledge of skills that other students and graduates list. Get help. Your **Step 2** list may well surprise you at the skills you have long held or recently developed. You may, in other words, already be developing the confidence that effective job searching entails.

Common and Uncommon Skills

Don't sell yourself short when listing your skills. You probably have more and different skills than you immediately realize. Some of the common skills that lawyers possess include oral advocacy, written advocacy, legal research, document drafting, interviewing, counseling, consultation, negotiation, leadership, work management, and problem solving. Specialized skills that some lawyers possess include scholarship editing and publication, legislative research, drafting legislation, administrative research, drafting regulations, case management, risk management, data analysis, patent research and construction, policy development, mediation, arbitration, systems analysis, and staff supervision. Lawyers may also have special expertise in areas such as employment law, labor law, benefits law, securities law, financial regulation, insurance law, health law, healthcare compliance, construction litigation, real-estate development, real-estate financing, municipal financing, transportation regulation, mergers and acquisitions, commercial law, bankruptcy, computer law, disabilities law, education law, and so on. Technology skills that lawyers commonly possess include word processing, document assembly, electronic communications, electronic filing, document search, presentation, and spreadsheet use. Some lawyers have special technology skills around publishing, website development, social media, illustration, and animation. Cast your net widely as you list your skills and areas of expertise. If you find listing your skills too great a challenge, then try thinking of *data* skills like organizing and interpreting, *people* skills like counseling and persuading, and *items* skills like constructing and installing. Build a broad list of your skills.

Don't Just List—Analyze

As you make your skills list, analyze it. Identify your strongest skills representing the areas where you feel that you would outperform other qualified candidates. Write, "My strongest skills are...." Analyze your list for the skills that truly distinguish you, adding, "The skills that most distinguish me are...." Also, identify your average skills that qualify you as competent but that do not distinguish you from other qualified candidates. Be ready to let employers know that you have those average skills, but don't be so ready to tout them if indeed those skills are just ordinary skills that don't distinguish you from other candidates. Bragging about skills that every qualified candidate has does you no good and probably instead causes employers to question your overall skill level. Here in your **Step 2** journal entries, don't hesitate to identify weaknesses. Be frank about your weaknesses, but also be generous to yourself about your strengths. Look at your law school grades, co-curricular and extra-curricular programs, and pro bono and clinical experiences for where you did best. Think of professors, lawyers, and employers who lauded you about certain skills, habits, practices, disciplines, and performances. Build yourself up to the point that you know what you do well. Distinguish your *learned* skills from your *natural* skills, emphasizing both in your job search, showing that you have natural strengths but can also acquire new skills. Analyze which skills *transfer* well from job to job and task to task. Identify especially those skills that you have already shown that you believe will transfer best to your preferred law job. Highlight those transferable skills, and describe them as such. Identify *adaptive* skills that show how well you can change what you do to accommodate new demands and adjust to new systems. Label those adaptive skills as such, and highlight them in your job-search resources, job applications, and interviews. You will repeatedly use your skills analysis to identify, qualify, distinguish, and promote yourself.

Remediate Your Skills

Your skills analysis will also spur you to get better where you need to do so. Job search can include not only looking for the job that you need but also preparing yourself better to get the job that you want. Yes, you were thinking of just going out and getting the dream job without first doing anything further. Yet once you analyze your skills and evaluate the job market (which is the next step), you may find that you lack just one or two skills or qualifications for that dream job. You may also find that you are able to readily acquire those skills and attain those qualifications, not in a year or two of expensive further education but rather in just a week or few weeks of study, practice, and action. Lawyers often go to weekend or week-long conferences coming back with expert knowledge and resources that they can quickly turn into distinguishing skills and expertise. Other lawyers attend two-day and three-day trainings or workshops that quickly build new skills. Some of those conferences, trainings, and workshops or other professional-development opportunities offer full-ride or partial-ride scholarships to law students, new lawyers, or relatively indigent lawyers. You may also still have time to register for one of your law school's elective courses or even to audit a law school course at reduced tuition, or to participate in a journal, competition, or other co-curricular or extra-curricular activity to build your skills. Don't underestimate your opportunity to acquire new knowledge, skills, and expertise quickly and inexpensively. One of the more-fruitful actions that you can take toward getting a job is to remediate gaps in your skills after you have closely analyzed them.

Internships Build Skills

An internship is among the best of ways not only to acquire or remediate skills but also to test whether you have them while also proving that you can acquire them or have acquired them. Law students must have clinical experience to graduate. You get that experience either in a law school clinic or an internship at a

19

remote site, usually a law firm, where you can do legal work under a lawyer's supervision, also with faculty oversight. Law school clinics are excellent ways to build skills including not only interviewing, counseling, and court representation but also management skills like intake procedures, file set up, and case-management systems. Law-firm internships are often not as structured or systematic in their skills instruction as a law school clinic. Yet internships can have an advantage in helping you focus your skill development on what a specific employer, your internship site, needs you to do. You may end up with a job offer at the end of the internship. Even if not, then you may end up with a strong recommendation letter touting that you have acquired specific skills. If you pursue an internship, then be sure that the experience does build skills that you need to learn and prove for future employment. Investigate and choose the internship carefully to ensure that it will build the skills that you desire. Then conduct yourself to ensure that you are acquiring those skills. As soon as you find yourself in an internship routine that you already know and perform well, ask your field supervisor for other work that will help you build new skills. Enlist your faculty supervisor if the field supervisor does not understand or appreciate the internship's educational goals and nature. Educate and invent yourself through your internship. Don't simply become a cog in someone else's wheel.

Cross-Cultural Competence

Consider cross-cultural competence as an example of a skill that you may possess, from which your job search would benefit by its advertisement, or that you may need to analyze and even remediate. The nation has seen substantial immigration, producing a population more diverse than in prior generations. Many employers recognize the need both to hire a more-diverse workforce and also to serve a more-diverse client population with a workforce having cross-cultural sensitivities and skills. The law profession has a special interest in both more-diverse hiring and skills more supportive of diverse clients because of its unique role in ensuring access to opportunity. You may or may not count yourself as diverse, although that question, too, is one that you ought to analyze. Diversity comes on multiple measures, not just sex or ethnicity. Employers independently value cross-cultural skills, whether or not you are a member of a population that an employer would consider to increase its workforce's diversity. Your education, training, or experience may have given you cross-cultural skills. Law schools and other educational programs are deliberate in offering courses and training in cross-cultural competence, and foreign study, pro bono, volunteer, or other experiences from which you can gain and within which you can demonstrate those skills. If you have already resorted to those courses and programs, or have other demonstrable basis on which to claim cross-cultural skills, then you should consider how to reflect that experience and those skills. If you do not have those skills, then you may be able to take a course or training, or engage in a program or activity, through which you can relatively quickly acquire and demonstrate those skills or rudiments of them. You may not be fluent or conversational in Spanish, for instance, but an experience abroad or locally might demonstrate or hone your ability to navigate and relate using basics of that language or other languages. And cross-cultural competence goes well beyond knowledge of another language. Analyze and if appropriate build and remediate your cross-cultural and other marketable skills.

Write Your Own Profile

To evaluate whether you have adequately confirmed your commitments in **Step 1** and articulated your skills in **Step 2**, try writing your own one-paragraph professional profile. Lawyers and other professionals often do get to write their own bios. Imagine, for instance, that you have written a book, book chapter, or article for which the publisher needs to include your brief bio. Or imagine that you are presenting at a professional conference for which the organizers need to list your brief professional bio or that you have joined the volunteer board of a charitable organization that wants to tout your expertise along with the expertise of other board members. Or better yet, imagine that your new law firm asks you to write a paragraph about yourself as a professional, for the firm to post on your website page along with details of your resume and practice areas. What in concise form would you want others to hear or read about you for the first time, as an overview of who you are or want to be as a lawyer and professional? Write that paragraph-long bio in the third person, describing yourself as you hope that someone else would see and describe you. Write your bio into **Step 2** of your electronic job-search journal. Return to your bio from time to time to improve it, especially as you think of challenges that you have overcome, core commitments that you hold, and goals that you have achieved or hope to achieve. Brainstorm and cluster your thoughts until your bio has a theme. Let your **Step 2** bio become your elevator speech, that brief self-description that you would give instantly if someone asked about your interests and background.

STEP 3:

Evaluate Your Job Market

Your Job Market Matters

Admit that when you begin to look for a job, you think about yourself first, not the employer who is looking for you. You need to change that approach or, if not change it, then at least *supplement* it. Strange as it may seem, you need to be thinking about the employer who is looking for you, not just what you want out of the employment. The reason that you need to be thinking about what employers want is that jobs arise out of a labor market. Any job searcher would like to find a job ready-made for the applicant, exactly what the applicant first envisioned when beginning a job search and perfectly suited to the applicant's needs and preferences. Well, guess what? We don't get to figuratively dream up our jobs and then have employers come and hire us for them. That's not how job hunting works. Employers, not prospective employees, establish the job qualifications. In the labor market, employees influence wages, benefits, and other conditions of work. If an employer can't find anyone to work at low wages, with poor benefits, or with long and inflexible hours, then the employer will have to sweeten the proverbial pot. But employers still determine job descriptions, skills, and qualifications. Employers know what they need to get the job done. You will find your job at the intersection of who you are, including the commitments that you discerned in **Step 1** and the skills that you articulated in **Step 2**, and what employee your future employer needs, as you discover that need in this **Step 3** evaluating the job market.

Research the Job Market

Record in **Step 3** of your job-search journal everything that you learn about your relevant job market. Learning about the job market should be an early step in your job search. You may still need to do a lot of work on **Step 1** commitments or **Step 2** skills when you hear or otherwise learn something about the job market. You should devote time and attention early in your job search to researching the job market, beginning with a visit to your law school's career office. A career-planning appointment with your law school's career counselor is your number one research activity. Yet you will also continue to learn tips about the job market throughout your job search. Record them in your job-search journal's **Step 3** whenever you learn them. Capture now what you just learned. A friend who just got a job, the staff person in your school's career office, or a lawyer mentor may give you a tip about the market, like a certain subject field or geographic area is hot. If so, then record the market information right then. Record what you discern right now. Let your research accumulate over time so that you have more data from which to draw helpful conclusions. When you systematically record the individual discrete tips and tidbits, you gain a picture that no one tip would show. Focus on the skills, education, and experience that employers may be seeking, but also include information about currently growing law fields, general economic trends, and trends specific to the geographic area or areas in which you are focusing your job search. Refer to your job-market research whenever your activities do not seem to be producing results, whenever you seem to have reached dead ends. Adjust your activities to reflect realities of the job market.

Evaluate the Job Market

As you record job-search information, try to evaluate how the information and patterns that you discern are shaping the job market. For instance, you may read about significant growth in the demand for lawyers skilled in healthcare compliance and health-insurance regulation. If so, then don't simply assume that you would need relevant coursework, research experience, clinical experience, or other special qualifications in that specific field to find a job in some way related to the market's new demand. Sure, if you were already a healthcare-compliance expert, then you may well find a job, although you probably are not such an expert. Yet you may also discern through further research that few if any lawyers are already experts in the emerging law that makes for the hot new field. The relevant expertise may have more to do with administrative law than healthcare. You might have ignored the hot new field because you had no health-industry education, training, or experience, when instead you may have had exactly had exactly the kind of coursework, research experience, or clinical experience in administrative law to qualify you for the field. For another example, you may hear that the dominant industry in your geographic area is shrinking quickly. While you might correctly assume that the market for law services to that industry is shrinking with it, your further research might show a corresponding *increase* in small-business startups, bankruptcies, divorces, employment litigation, benefits litigation, and other related law-practice fields. The point here is to *evaluate* the results that your job-market research produces, not simply to record the information.

Conventional Research Sources

You may wonder how to research a job market. You may even think that law school didn't train you for *this* kind of research, as if somehow job research rather than legal research is beneath you. Your law school's career office, or your law library's reference librarians, will guide you to conventional research sources. You may believe those conventional sources to be too widely known and available, not sufficiently targeted or specific to your interests, or even too stale and not reflective of the current market. Yet don't overlook those conventional sources. Even general sources like the *Dictionary of Occupational Titles, Occupational Outlook Handbook*, and *Guide for Occupational Exploration* can give you important context for more-specific and more-recent information that you find in targeted sources. The federal *Dictionary of Occupational Titles* has a companion online *Occupational Information Network* (known as the O*Net) that helps you assess your skills against the many listed occupations. Many states also offer online *Career Information Systems* that list the vast majority of jobs in the state and associated *Micro-Skills Programs* that analyze the skills associated with each job category. You can focus your research in these conventional sources on law and law-related jobs while also comparing and contrasting those jobs with jobs in other fields.

Lawyer Research Sources

You may not find ready access to the above conventional and general resources, or may not have the interest or success in exploring them. Whether or not those conventional and general sources are productive be sure to research sources within the law field. Within the law field, lawyer job-market research is everywhere, in nearly every professional journal or other source that you may pick up. Skilled lawyers, including those who are fully employed and have no need of looking for other jobs, use those market research sources all of the time to confirm, develop, expand, and alter their existing practices. Pick up the latest lawyer magazine or newspaper, or read the endless online lawyer journals, news sources, social-media accounts, blog sites, and websites. Stories and information abound in those sources on new practice areas, hot practice fields, new management practices, new technologies, new law firms and practice groups, and new practice products and services. Every national, state, and local lawyer periodical has articles, advertisements, notices, and information in other forms that show the fields, locales, industries, and other categories and patterns in which lawyers are working or not working. Whether or not the authors and contributors of those writings were thinking of the job market doesn't matter. These stories and information sources give you important job-market clues. They tell you what lawyers are doing and not doing these days, not in tables of government statistics but instead hot off the presses in readily digestible form. Read what lawyers read, and you will learn what lawyers are doing, which means that you will learn where lawyers are employed.

Informational Interviews

Another great job-market research activity involves communicating with lawyers who actively practice in the fields in which you would like to find employment. Anytime that you speak with a lawyer, whether informally at a professional gathering, with an adjunct professor before or after class, socially over coffee or a meal, or in any other setting, you have an opportunity for what placement professionals call an *informational interview*. Informational interviews can produce a trove of job-market information. Never miss the opportunity to ask the lawyers with whom you come into contact about the job market. Beyond specifically asking about jobs, also ask about practice areas, hot fields, fields that are shrinking or growing, firms that are adding or laying off lawyers, new practice groups that firms are looking to add, and any other market information. Nearly every lawyer whom you ask will give you some opinion, whether positive or negative, about certain aspects of the job market. Don't take negative information too negatively. Lawyers (and other professionals) like to grumble even during good times. See below in this same **Step 3** the paragraph on negative research results for good reasons to value negative evaluations of the job market. Listen especially, though, for tips on what fields, locales, services, practices, practice groups, and industries are growing.

Many lawyers have excess work, ten or twenty percent more work than they can handle. Those lawyers are often very conscious of the source and trend or direction of their extra work. Even if not, then your curiosity may help them momentarily examine it, in which instance they may well disclose it to you. Record that information in **Step 3** of your electronic job-search journal so that it can guide you later. You may use that information later to pursue specific job opportunities or to impress an employer with your knowledge of practice-development and growth opportunities. Informational interviews can also lead you directly to job openings. Few practices have such great value as informational interviews, particularly if you are able to locate the most-active lawyers who stay most abreast of developments in the field. And don't overlook opportunities to conduct informational interviews with other professionals who work with lawyers. They can be other good sources of job-market research.

Conducting Informational Interviews

Conducting an informational interview can (and probably should) be informal and even relaxing, lighthearted, social, and fun. People generally appreciate when you take an interest in them. You may know the traditional approach to conversation which is to first speak about the weather, then about family or recreation, and only then about something more serious including the conversation's purpose or point. Professionals are no different. You can make small talk with a lawyer including about the weather or recreation, such as whether the lawyer skis, golfs, or travels. Despite the confidences with which lawyers must hold client matters, you can also *talk shop* with a lawyer. Lawyers are skilled at holding conversations about work that do not reveal confidences. While you don't want to pry with specific questions like *what was your gross revenue* or *who is your best client*, you can certainly without offense ask a lawyer's practice field, practice mix (combination of different fields that work well together), most-creative or enjoyable work, and most-challenging work or issue.

28

You can also ask what firms might be looking for in any new labor that they hire, such as specialty coursework, specialty skills, or even character profiles. For instance, some surveys indicate that firms value very highly a new associate's ability to engender client confidence. Listen to what the lawyers whom you interview say not only about hot practice fields but also about professional conduct and character. Use that research and insight to develop and refine your resume and cover letter, and to choose your best writing sample. And don't forget to ask the lawyer or other professional whom you interview, with whom else they think you should speak. That practice is networking.

Job Postings

Actual job postings should be a primary job-research source. The job-market information that you discern from other sources is indirect, implicit, and general information. That indirect information can be very significant, especially for open opportunities that employers are not actually posting in traditional forums. Yet job postings are the real thing. A job posting generally means that the employer intends to fill that specific position based on the listed qualifications within a reasonably short time. Your law school will have job listings. Many online sites such as LinkedIn provide job listings. Local and state bar associations often also do so. Reviewing job listings regularly, and even researching archives and databases of old job listings, can give you a reliable picture of who is hiring for what jobs. Of course, when you identify an open position that meets your job criteria and for which you qualify, then apply as **Step 8** below addresses. Yet when you review job postings, don't review them solely for openings in which you may be interested and for which you qualify. Remember that **Step 3** is about job-market research. For instance, you may discover from reviewing old, archived postings that the same jobs with the same qualifications, *ones for which you qualify,* tend to keep coming up. You may not find a current listing for one of those jobs, but from your research you may anticipate that one is likely to open soon. Indeed, you may realize that employers probably currently need to fill such positions but just haven't posted them yet. Those likely open but not-posted positions should then become the ones for you to pursue. Job-market research can prove critical to your success.

Research Goal

Remember that job-search research isn't all about finding that one job for which to apply. Whether or not you actually find a specific job in your job-search research for which you intend to apply may be significantly less important than the patterns and other information that you discover from your job-search research. As just indicated in the prior paragraph, lots of hiring occurs, in some fields the vast majority of hiring, without job postings. Employers should post jobs widely, especially to ensure inclusive candidate pools. Many employers do not do so. While courts and other government agencies will routinely post all openings, many other employers, especially law firms, prefer to hire by word of mouth, through networking. They may wish to avoid letting other firms know that they are looking to add one or more lawyers, for competitive reasons, to avoid gossip, and to minimize awkward inquiries judges, lawyers, and other professionals with whom they have standing relationships. Law firms may have internal reasons not to publicize an opening, such as the imminent need to replace a lawyer about whose departure the lawyer or other lawyers in the firm do not yet know. Firms may also simply wish to avoid receiving multiple inquiries and resumes. When you research the job market, you are finding network leads more so than actual job postings. The goal of your job-market research is not specific job postings. Your goal is to identify market opportunities that you can investigate by other means, not to locate specific open jobs, although don't be surprised if the latter happens for you, too. One good thing leads to another.

Negative Research Results

Just as importantly, record your research tips and results *whether positive or negative.* For instance, you may notice from reviewing multiple job listings that they all seem to share a similar qualification, perhaps for a certain number of years of experience. You may learn that you do not have the experience that the job market for the kind of job that you would like to find appears to require. Some employers prefer to hire new lawyers who have never worked anywhere else, giving the employer the chance to train the new lawyer in the employer's unique procedures and to avoid all conflicts of interest. Other employers, especially in certain fields (in some cases like civil litigation) or settings (in some cases like in-house counsel) prefer to hire lawyers with at least two, five, or even ten years of experience. If you cannot meet the experience requirement for jobs of the kind that you are most interested in finding and for which you are otherwise qualified, then you will need to either (a) show prospective employers why they should hire you anyway, (b) get the experience first before seeking those jobs, or (c) find a job in a different area. To determine your next step, you may even need to do more market research and testing, such as contacting one or more of those employers to see how serious they are about the experience requirement. The point here is that negative information is just as valuable and often much more valuable than positive information. Negative information can help you remediate weaknesses in your qualifications when possible but can also help you not waste your precious job-search time when you cannot meet job requirements that certain parts of the job market demand.

Identify and Pursue Trends

Throughout your research, look for trends. You only need one job offer. Broad, national or even international trends may have no impact at all on the one job offer that you need. On the other hand, trends arise by aggregating individual data. Every documented trend reflects real jobs lost or gained in the job market. If your research indicates that a certain law field or geographic area is on a downward trend and further indicates good reason to believe that the trend will accelerate or continue, then you may want to spend more time looking for a job in a different field or area. You might still find a job in the downward-trending field or area, but if you did, then you would probably want to investigate carefully the security associated with that job before accepting its offer. Use trends to target your job search. For example, one of the broadest trends involves the aging law profession, consistent with the accelerating retirement of the baby-boom generation. An aging workforce can threaten law firms of any size, large or small, in their continuity, currency, creativity, vitality, productivity, and compensation structure. If you discern that a law firm's hiring you would address that substantial concern, then you might target your applications to those aging firms and shape your job-application materials to reflect your relative youth and, more significantly, your currency, creativity, vitality, and productivity. Alternatively, you might just go find one of the many solo practitioners who hope soon to retire, investigating the possibility of working for or with the solo practitioner to take over the practice. Look for demographic trends like immigration and diversification, industry trends like new oil-and-gas exploration, economic trends affecting banking and investment, and even service-delivery and workforce-organization trends like alternative compensation structures, outsourcing, and contract services. Look even for current events, like natural catastrophes, political movements, legislative reforms, or technology revolutions that may imminently spark new trends. Then pursue new opportunities that take advantage of those emerging or imminent trends. And even if you cannot discern a trend in a manner that enables you to pursue it, at least be aware of when your conventional job-search routines and targets are fighting or riding a trend. If nothing else, then trends can tell you why you may be drilling proverbial dry holes and need to move your effort elsewhere.

Solo Practitioners

Much of the above discussion remains true even if you intend or expect to become a solo practitioner rather than find an employer to offer you a job. Solo practitioners don't get to just dream up the clients and then have those clients come to buy services. Even solo practitioners must be aware of the needs for their services. Some solos prepare to serve one client market but soon find out that the demand for services is in a slightly or grossly different market, which is all to the good if the solo can quickly adjust to the demand. Lawyers in solo practice and law firms constantly adjust to changing demand. Lawyers frequently start practice doing one thing but end up doing others. Changing practice areas, geographic locales, and service-delivery structures over time is certainly no shame. Outstanding lawyers in one field can become outstanding lawyers in another field over time. One of the most common questions that lawyers ask one another when renewing old acquaintances is *so what are you doing most of these days?* Yet you would do better to prepare yourself now to serve clients who need your services rather than to adjust later when you discover that prospective clients don't need the services that you initially offered. Job-market research can teach you much of what you need to know not just about the lawyer jobs out there but also the *clients* who are out there. Jobs go hand in hand with clients. Solos simply discover faster than other lawyers who the clients are and what they need from lawyers. No matter the nature and goal of your job search, value job-market research. Research teaches you about clients. Indeed, here's a helpful thought: don't stop your job-market research with your first job. Keep pursuing the clients. Serving them is why you got a law license. The job is only the medium, while effective and fruitful client service is the goal. Prospective employers appreciate that perspective, too, keeping your focus on clients.

Specific Employer Information

You should also plan for finding out about specific employers, particularly those employers who express interest in hiring you. Just because you receive a job offer doesn't mean that you should take it. You should have some confidence that the offered job will be a good fit for both you and the employer. Researching specific employers before they express any interest in hiring you could be a waste of precious time. But you should have a sense of the information that you would want to know about those employers and how you can research that information during the hiring process. Interviews are an example. Interviews can and should involve an exchange of information. You don't just share your own qualifications but can and should also be learning about the employer and position. If you haven't discerned in advance what you need to know, then you won't do a good job of researching when the opportunity for a job with a specific employer arises. During an interview, you can ask the employer's representatives for information about the employer and job. Yet you can also perform research both before and after the interview using various other methods and sources. Websites, web searches, public filings, and informational interviews with law professors, lawyers, and others who know the employer can help you discern which employers make the best fit for you. Make your research both general as to the market and specific as to the employer.

STEP 4:

Develop Your Resources

Your Resources Matter

None of us is an open book. We share with others only those of our attributes and experiences that we wish to share, while hiding other predilections, preferences, and affinities. Especially, we all tend to put our proverbial best foot forward when trying to appeal to potential employers. We publicize our successes and strengths, not our weaknesses and failures. Employers, of course, expect us to do so. Yet nearly all employers of any size have had some experience with hiring a poor fit. Nearly all employers have had that *if-we'd-only-known* experience of regretting that they hadn't learned more before making an ill-fitting hire. Employers face a challenge in learning about you and other candidates for hire. Appreciate how significant that challenge is for employers. Discern how you can help employers meet that challenge. Employers will not hire candidates about whom they have insufficient information. In competitive job markets, the burden of proving that you fit the job is on you, not the employer. To help employers discover what they need to know about you to make a hiring offer, in **Step 4** of your job-search journal, list every job-search resource that you have acquired or developed, or need to acquire or develop, to prove your fitness for hire. Job-search

35

resources are those things that represent who you are, what you have done, what skills you have, and what others think of you.

Your Resume

Traditionally, your primary job-search resource would have been a resume. Although many traditions have changed with the advent of online job-recruiting technology, for lawyers a resume remains your foundational opening document, the tool that you use to encourage interested employers to take the next step with you in the hiring process. Without a resume, you may not stand much chance of getting your foot in the door with many potential employers. Even for well-known candidates, employers need a resume on file for administrative purposes and also to share with others who do not know the candidate. If your college-roommate best friend knew of an opening at your friend's law firm, then your friend would still need your resume to share with the firm's other lawyers. You should have been developing your resume from Day One of law school. A resume basically lists your accomplishments, not just where you have been but also what you *did* there to distinguish yourself. Your resume will certainly list your college or university and law school, with your undergraduate and any graduate degrees including your law degree, and prior substantial work experience. But you should also be thinking about what you *accomplished* in your educational programs and work experiences. Be ready to list not just awards and honors but also completed projects, innovations, and even team accomplishments in which you shared. Yet a resume is not just to get a job. A resume is also an assessment tool helping you see what you have accomplished but also what you need yet to accomplish. For instance, if you cannot list on your resume any volunteer activity or other community involvement, then you may need to volunteer, serve, and get involved. The point is that you should develop a sound and impressive resume from the start, using your draft resume as an assessment tool.

Resume Themes

In a truly open job-recruiting process, where the employer has no particular inside preferred candidate ready to fill the job, employers use resume reviews to sort not only qualified from unqualified but also more-desirable from less-desirable candidates. Your resume alone may determine whether you make the first cut, and in only a reviewer's twenty-second average review. In that case, you obviously should give considerable thought and effort to the immediate impression, both substantive and procedural or form, your resume conveys. While class rank, service awards, prior employment, competitions, publications, and other recognition, accomplishments, and events convey their own sense of substance, you can amplify that sense by discerning and executing a deliberate resume theme. In your **Step 4** electronic job-search journal, reflect on and record your best themes. Your theme may indeed be accomplishments, like *look at all I've already done*, particularly if your accomplishments in fact do stand out. Or your theme may be skills, like *look at all that I can do*, particularly if your skills in fact do stand out. Or your theme may be knowledge, like *look at all that I already know*, particularly if you have specialty knowledge, perhaps from your undergraduate education or substantial work in another field. Or your theme may be service, like *look at all that I want to do*, particularly if you have already demonstrated substantial service commitments as a volunteer, in charitable and community work, or perhaps in military service. Develop your own theme, and then work to make your resume reflect it. Also, pay close attention to the procedural, form, or format impressions that your resume leaves. Resumes should above all be clear, concise, and communicative. Leave appropriate white space and at least three-quarter-inch margins, rather than cramming everything in. Review many examples, produce and refine many drafts, and get your career office's review and help.

Resume Types

Reviewers see two general types of resumes. The chronological resume emphasizes your sequential education and work experience in order from oldest to most recent, followed by service activities and special language or technology skills. The functional resume lists your job objective, summary characteristics, and skills analysis, followed by employment, education, activities, and languages or skills. Notice that the two resume types have most of the same factual information, just that the chronological resume emphasizes history and continuity, while the functional resume emphasizes skills. Job candidates tend to use the chronological resume if they have continuous education and work history, and seek a job in the same field. Job candidates tend to use the functional resume if they have discontinuous education or work history (gaps in either or both) or seek a job in a different field. That said, reviewers, especially in the highly traditional law profession, generally find the chronological resume easier to read and interpret quickly, and thus more traditional and trustworthy. Functional resumes, while potentially more helpful to the employer's actual needs and more illustrative of your actual skills, can confuse or discourage a traditional reviewer, and even cause a reviewer to question the candidate's ability and willingness to conform to conventions and show candor as to qualifications. If you believe that a functional resume would better show your skills, then consider using the traditional chronological form but developing its entries to show your associated skills in functional form. Also, use your cover letter to highlight your skills and objective.

Resume Details

Don't miss important details when preparing your resume. Your first and last names should appear at the resume's top in larger font than anything else on the resume. Use your current legal name. Middle names and initials are optional. List your current address below your name, the address at which you would receive mail promptly, even if your permanent or legal addresses are elsewhere, such as back home. Below your address, list the telephone number at which the employer can most quickly reach you, typically your cell phone. Below or next to your telephone number, list your email address, typically your law school email. Avoid using a personal email address with an unconventional identifier such as *hotshot@renegade.com*. If you have already taken and passed a bar exam, and received your law license, then indicate under a next section titled *Bar Admission* the state bar and date or year of your licensure. If you are not yet licensed, then you may indicate the bar and exam for which you have registered. Next, in your resume's *Education* section, list your law school, city and state, juris-doctor degree, and year of degree, or if not yet earned, then anticipated year of degree but clearly marking that degree as *expected* or *anticipated*. Include your law school grade-point average only if above 3.00/4.00 and class rank only if in the top quartile or third. Also include Dean's List, Honor Roll, Order of the Coif, Law Review, Certificates of Merit, and other academic or service honors. Consider including program certificates, student-organization leadership, competition participation or wins, and even elective coursework, particularly if related to the position for which you are applying. List the same basic information, grade point, and academic honors as to your four-year undergraduate degree, including major, and other graduate degrees that you have earned, but without substantial additional detail. Do not list your high school diploma, any associate's degrees that you earned, or any colleges or universities that you attended without earning a degree.

Other Resume Sections

After your bar licensure and education, you should next list your *Legal Experience*, meaning both paid and unpaid roles doing legal work for a lawyer or organization providing legal services. List the most-recent experience first. Include the name of the organization, your title or role, the dates you fulfilled that role, and action phrases describing what you did. You should include your law school clinic experience or internship experience here, in addition to pro bono service and research or teaching assistant experience. Also include any associated recognition that you earned. You may then list *Other Experience*, particularly if your legal experience is limited and your other experience is substantial and significant to your future law career. As to other experience, list your employers, title or position, employment dates, and city and state, in the same reverse chronological order (most recent first) that you used for your education and legal experience. Again, include action phrases describing what you did relative to each significant experience, particularly if the work qualifies you for special consideration for the position for which you applied. In following sections, you may choose to list *Language Skills* indicating whether fluent or basic, special *Technology Skills*, professional *Memberships*, *Community Service*, other licenses or certifications, and publications, presentations, or conference attendance but only if related to the position that you are pursuing.

Multiple Resumes

Indeed, you may find yourself wanting to develop more than one resume. Go ahead and do so. Do not hesitate to have multiple resumes, each for a different job field or type of job. In **Step 4**, list the different resumes that you may need to develop, for instance, for a large-firm versus a small-firm job, or for an in-house or agency position instead, or in the family law field versus in a business start-up role. You may have coursework, publications, memberships, awards, or service activities that make perfect sense for one role but have no connection with another role. You may have qualified yourself well for two entirely different positions. You need not have a single resume that attempts to split the difference between the two positions, winning you neither of them. Instead, develop two resumes, one for each position for which you qualified yourself. Of course, every representation that you make about yourself in any resume should be completely accurate and in no way misleading. The bad consequences of any misrepresentation can be career-long and devastating to reputation. Your resume must not portray you as you wish to be but instead as you are. Do not exaggerate. Yet you have probably been many different things to many different persons and organizations during the course of your education, employment, and other experience. You probably have at least some latitude, and possibly significant latitude, to develop alternative resumes that communicate your skills and attributes differently to different employers. Not all law jobs are the same. Discern the different connections between you and those different jobs, and then make your multiple different resumes reflect those connections.

Electronic Resumes

Many employers, particularly those with open, online application processes that invite and receive many applications, require electronic resume submission. Those employers are increasingly likely to use an electronic search system to cull preferred candidates from among the many applications. In those instances, no one will have looked at your resume. You make or miss the cut for many jobs simply based on the words that such a system discovers in your resume. Some of those employers require you to submit your electronic resume as an attachment in a specific file format. Be sure to comply strictly with any such requirement, or the system may well reject your application without notice to you. Other employers using electronic review may require you to copy and paste your resume into your email reply or an online application box. Deliberately reformat your print-copy resume into an electronic-submission version in order to comply with those email-reply or online-submission requirements. Remove tabs or other formatting so that all entries left justify in the email body or online box. Single space entries, but double space between major entries for clarity. Remove bullets that email or online fonts won't replicate, using hyphens or asterisks instead. Do not worry about keeping the online resume to one page because online scrolling won't show pagination. Before sending the resume in your job application, send it to yourself in an email, confirming that you have fixed any format errors or anomalies. Be sure that the electronic resume that you transmit has the clear, concise, readable, and error-free content and format that electronic communications support. Don't send something that you later learn didn't transmit in the form that you intended.

Electronic Resume Keywords

Then, before sending, examine your electronic resume to ensure that it uses appropriate action, experience, and skill words, and practice fields, describing your qualifications. Make as sure as you can that the employer's electronic-review system recognizes the words that you use to describe your qualifications, particularly when your qualifications seem to fit especially well the position for which you are applying. Think carefully about why your qualifications fit so well, choosing those words that make the connection between your education, skill, and experience — in other words, your *resume* — and the employer's job description. For example, if you are applying for a healthcare law position, then your electronic resume should include health-field-related words such as *medical, hospital, health, clinical, physician, nurse,* and *biology* or *anatomy,* that accurately describe your qualifications. If you also have special research skill or doctrinal knowledge in peculiar healthcare-law-related issues like the federal physician-referral law that lawyers know as *Stark,* the federal health-insurance law known as the *Affordable Care Act* or *ACA,* or the federal patient-confidentiality law known as *HIPAA,* then be sure to use those words in your healthcare-law electronic resume. If you are applying for a tax law position, then your electronic resume should include tax- and accounting-related words, such as *tax, accounting, C.P.A., certified, finance, financial, compliance,* and *analysis* or *analyst,* that accurately describe your qualifications. Your electronic resume for an estate-planning position might include words like *estate, planning, probate, family, tax, will, trust,* and *guardian* or *conservator,* if you have qualifications those words describe. Don't overlook attributes that employers may highly value, like *teamwork, civility, professional* or *professionalism,* and *integrity,* assuming that you have accomplishments that reflect those attributes. Even for a general-practice or small-firm position, or where you otherwise don't know of any specific employer priorities other than general competence as a lawyer, your electronic resume might include skill words like *trial, negotiation, interviewing, intake, communication,* and *consulting,* or practice-management terms like *systems, management, billing, files, docket,* and *marketing, branding, growth,* or *development,* again assuming that you have those qualifications. As you think about what might alert an electronic search, you are also honing your resume to the eyes of a human reviewer. After all, someone at the employer wrote the electronic search terms.

Your Cover Letter

Traditionally, candidates would convey their resume under a cover letter, making the cover letter another primary job-search resource. Even when conveying a resume as an attachment to an email rather than by postal mail, job candidates routinely and properly also attach a cover letter with the email. In doing so, a candidate ensures that if the employer prints out the resume to circulate to reviewers, the cover letter is likely to accompany the resume. Candidates may also use abbreviated portions of the contents of a cover letter in the email message itself. Cover letters enable a candidate to highlight accomplishments, express specific interest in the employer and position, and demonstrate professional communication skill. Don't wait to draft your first cover letter until you find a job for which you want to apply. If you don't have a cover letter ready now for the job that you want to find, then draft it now. Drafting the cover letter may teach you something about yourself, your qualifications, your resume and resources, or the job itself. Also, when you do find the job for which you want to apply and you open the electronic cover letter that you drafted earlier, you will very likely see ways to improve it before adding the employer and address, and sending it out. You will, in other words, have made one or more thoughtful drafts and then improved on the last draft, making for a better cover letter. As in the case of resumes, don't stop at one cover letter. Draft multiple cover letters, each for a different job for which you hope to apply. Then, when you find that open job position, you will be ready with a well-written, thoughtful cover letter. Cover letters can be hard to write on the spur of the moment, so write drafts early. Cover letters can be particularly hard to write because of the strong convention, one that you should follow, to keep them to a single page. Writing clearly, concisely, and compellingly is harder and takes more time than writing casually and conversationally.

Cover Letter Form and Contents

Cover letters have a traditional form and traditional content. They should, for instance, be on the same paper as your resume, and generally use the same font and other style as your resume. While unique cover letters can catch attention, in seeking lawyer jobs, you generally best follow those traditions. Those who employ lawyers want to know if the lawyer candidate knows and can follow rules, protocols, and conventions. They also want to know if you can write well. Follow good-writing conventions in your cover letter by using active rather than passive voice, shorter rather than convoluted sentences, transition sentences and phrases, shorter paragraphs, and correct grammar, punctuation, and spelling. Readable, conversational style is better for a cover letter than overly stiff and formal style. Cover letters demonstrate not only writing, editing, and proofreading ability, but also ability and willingness to discern, acknowledge, and follow professional form and writing conventions. Review online cover-letter examples and examples from your law school's career office. Request your career officer's close review of your cover letter. In general, follow business-correspondence format as to things like beginning or heading with your return address, then the date, then the addressee and address, then a subject line *Re:*, and ending with a salutation, typically *Sincerely*. Follow these additional guidelines. First, write your own original letter rather than using a stock letter. You want to follow conventions but not be exactly like everyone else. Second, address your letter to a specific person rather than to an organization or firm. If you don't know the name of the specific person responsible for receiving job applications, then research the employer online. If you must do so, then contact the organization for the name of the hiring-committee chair or hiring partner. Next, address that person with *Dear Mr.* or *Dear Ms.* Then, in the first paragraph, state the reason for which you write including the position for which you are applying and how you learned of the position. End the first paragraph with a sentence about why you are interested in and qualified for the position. In the second paragraph, give any relevant specifics about your law school, law school standing or program, and graduate and bar-exam dates. You should then articulate one or two skills and one or two accomplishments to highlight, referring the reader to your resume. Finally, in the third paragraph, repeat your interest in the position while asking for an interview. Indicate your availability at a specific telephone or email for notice of that interview. Be gracious in ending the letter, thanking the reader for the attention and time. Although the letter is obviously about your interest, try to minimize the usage of the word *I* while maximizing references to the employer and its interests. And as with your resume, proofread, proofread, proofread.

Your Writing Sample

A writing sample is a third common, traditional job-search resource. Employers nearly always ask for a resume. Candidates very commonly use a cover letter to convey and supplement the resume. Yet employers also frequently ask for a writing sample to accompany the resume or a later stage in the candidate process. Even when employers don't ask for a writing sample, candidates may wish to include one or an excerpt of one. Now is the best time to prepare a writing sample, not when you find the specific job for which you want to apply, when you will find yourself busy with multiple other tasks. Inventory the writings that your law school curriculum required or enabled you to produce. From your coursework, particularly in skills and writing courses, you may have memoranda, motions, briefs, responses, discovery requests, draft legislation, contracts, wills, trusts, articles of incorporation, bylaws, articles, case comments, and opinion letters. Which of them would best serve as examples both of your research and writing skills and of your doctrinal knowledge within the particular field for which you plan to apply for a job? Ask your career office, writing professors, and faculty advisor to help you evaluate and present your best work. If your work is longer than ten pages, then excerpt the argument section or other section that shows your reasoning. Mark the excerpted sample clearly as such, as in a "five-page excerpt of a twenty-page brief." If a key writing sample that you hope to use, such as something that you wrote at an internship, contains confidential client information, then remove all identifying information, and get the supervisor's written permission to use the no-longer-confidential document. If when you prepare the writing sample you feel as if you can improve it with edits, then do so unless the employer requests an unedited writing sample. When submitting the writing sample, explain in a brief cover sheet the course or program for which you prepared the writing sample, its original date as to when its law would be current, and the scope of and limitations on the assignment, such as that it involved research into only a certain state's law. As with your cover letter and resume, prepare multiple writing samples for each different type of job, if the different jobs that you are pursuing warrant different evidence of your writing expertise. Win with your writing sample.

Recommendation Letters

Recommendation letters remain a key traditional job-search resource. Some employers either require or encourage that you submit recommendation letters with your job-application materials. Others discourage or prohibit including supplemental resources like recommendation letters, at least until a later stage of the hiring process. Yet chances are good that those employers who find your cover letter, resume, and writing sample to qualify you for interview will soon require you to submit recommendation letters. Recommendation letters can be anything from as little as perfunctory to as much as powerful, depending on the author's knowledge of your character and experience, and the author's skill in and commitment to writing you a strong letter. Employers do sometimes disclose that a certain candidate got the job based on a recommendation letter when the candidate's resume, writing sample, or other resources would not have carried the day. Recommendation letters can be a make or break resource in your job search. Treat them that way. Develop strong professional relationships with influencers on whom you can later depend for a strong recommendation letter. Thoughtfully seek out those influencers, whether professors, deans, lawyers, judges, government officials, community representatives, industry representatives, or business persons, whose recommendation would impress employers in your preferred field. Seek recommendation letters from professors who know your academics, leadership, teamwork, writing, or skills, but also from clinic directors, internship supervisors, and other lawyers with whom you have worked and who know your work ethics, performance, and skills. When you ask for a recommendation letter, give the writer the name, title, employer, and address of the person to whom the writer should direct the letter. Also provide any job qualifications for the position you seek. Supply your resume along with a description of anything extra that you have done that your resume does not reflect but that might inform the writer. Don't hesitate to guide the writer as to the preferred contents of the letter. If the letter is general rather than for a specific position, then supply your general interests or preferred field or fields. Acquire multiple recommendation letters, deploying them strategically in your job search.

References

Having references available for your employer to contact is also a traditional job-search resource. Most candidates are not listing references on their resume but instead supplying references on the interested employer's request. Recommendation letters, rather than listing references on your resume, serve as your personal endorsement by influential evaluators. References thus usually become important only after your successful interview, when the employer has made an employment offer conditional on positive references or is seriously considering doing so. The late point in the hiring process when references usually become important doesn't mean that you should ignore references until later. Rather, start early in law school forming the relationships with your law professors, deans, and key staff, and with alumni and other lawyers and judges outside of the school, on whom you will later rely for references. As you approach your job search, review your law school and network contacts for those reference candidates who know you and your skills and character best, and who will be most likely to promote your candidacy. No one gets along with everyone. We all find acquaintances who like, trust, and respect us more than do other acquaintances. Choose your reference candidates from among those who most like, trust, and respect you. Then communicate with them about their willingness to serve as a reference. Listen carefully to their response to ensure that even if they are willing, they sound as if they will give you a strong positive reference. Do not assume that every person who agrees to serve as a reference will necessarily give you a positive review. If you choose unwisely, then you may find that your reference intentionally or unintentionally undermines your candidacy, even costing you the job. Choose professionals whom you feel that you can trust to serve this important function. Do not, though, choose close friends or family members, whom an employer would consider biased. Thank those professionals who agree to serve, even before they actually do serve, as your reference. Alert them when you have used their name so that they can provide you with any updated contact information and be ready for the call. Also, stay in touch with them even when you haven't used their name so that when you need to do so, they respect your request. When you supply an employer with requested references, include each reference's name, title, employer, business address, telephone including direct line or extension, and email address.

Professional Portfolios

If the cover letter, resume, writing sample, and recommendation letters are the meat and potatoes of job-search resources, then professional portfolios are the ice cream and cake. A professional portfolio collects, preserves, and presents evidence of who you are and what you can do as a professional. Portfolios, whether in print or online form, collect not only your cover letter, resume, recommendation letters, and multiple writing samples but can also include helpful evidence like your law school transcript, images of your undergraduate and law degrees, examples of your work, images of your recognitions and awards, documentation of your service work, and evaluations of your work. Listing on your resume an award of any kind impresses a reviewer, but actually seeing the handsome certificate in a color-printed or online image in your portfolio can convey additional helpful information and impressions. Listing on your resume certain volunteer, pro bono, or other service work conveys a level of community commitment, but actually seeing photographs of you doing that work with other volunteers, professionals, and service beneficiaries or recipients, in your portfolio, can simultaneously convey your teamwork and interaction skills, and service spirit. Listing competition participation or even a competition win can convey your performance skills, but actually seeing you counsel, negotiate, or advocate in a video recording of the competition reproduced in your portfolio can convey your outstanding demeanor, sensitivity, authority, or other performance skills. Seeing an excerpt of one writing sample conveyed with a resume under a cover letter can prove your writing skill, but reviewing excerpts of multiple writing samples in your portfolio can convey the breadth, depth, and consistency of your writing skill. Portfolios enable you to display more information in more different forms, with greater design and variation. Start your professional portfolio now, creating or acquiring evidence to place in it and developing it as you pursue your job search. Include in your professional portfolio evidence of your character, experiences, accomplishments, knowledge, and skills.

Presenting Your Portfolio

Your presentation portfolio differs from your professional portfolio in that you choose for your presentation portfolio only those things that you want a specific employer or group of similar employers to review. If you are providing a print copy of your portfolio, then make sure that it has a professional appearance in a binder or folder. Whether in print or online form, make sure that you organize your portfolio including a clear indication of its contents, either in a table of contents or opening cover letter, and with links or tabs for easy access to specific materials. Organization and legibility are critical because the portfolio represents not only what you have done but also the current quality of your presentation skills. Do not do a document dump. Employers will ignore a heavy, bulky, confusing, or inaccessible portfolio while holding its lack of organization and clarity against you. Choose no more than, say, the top ten to fifteen most-compelling pieces of evidence of your work. Make sure that your portfolio is current. Remove older work that no longer represents the higher quality of your skill. Backing up your job application at the appropriate moment with a presentation portfolio not only gives prospective employers the evidence that you want them to see but also gives you greater self-confidence. Use your presentation portfolio in informational interviews, too, if you find the chance. The lawyer or other professional with whom you meet may give you helpful feedback on it. You can also use your presentation portfolio for your own further assessment of whether you are ready for certain employment and how ready you appear.

Other Resources

Today, though, resumes, cover letters, writing samples, and recommendation letters, and even print or online portfolios, seem like only the iceberg's tip of job-search resources. Job candidates use many other tools beyond the traditional forms, to represent fully and fairly their job qualifications including their education, experiences, affinities, and expertise. Other job-search resources can include professional profiles and websites, blogs and blog sites, photographs and videos, and anything else that may promote your job search or that you may show to prospective employers to gain their confidence in you. An online portfolio, either confidential for your distribution only or in the form of an open online profile or website, can serve the same function as a portfolio, giving you a place to collect and organize evidence. and then also to even more conveniently share it through a link offered to prospective employers. Individual blogs that you have written and others have published, and blog sites that you have hosted, can be other easily shared resources establishing your credibility within online communities on certain expert subjects. A professional photograph, particularly one that appropriately conveys your professional attire and demeanor, and even your active engagement in a professional setting, can be worth a thousand words. A video excerpt of your mock-trial hearing, moot-court argument, or other competition performance, can be even more impressive and demonstrative evidence of your professional demeanor and comportment, and of your oral-advocacy skills. Use **Step 4** activities often and creatively. Refer to your **Step 4** job-search journal whenever you feel unqualified or unprepared. Let your job-search resources encourage and embolden you while you also spend time and creative effort developing additional resources. You very likely have more to offer employers than what your current resources adequately show.

Your Character and Skills Matter

Developing your job-search resources in **Step 4** is a critical step. Yet something equally important lies just behind that effort to generate traditional and non-traditional job-search resources. Resumes, cover letters, writing samples, and other job-search materials do not just write themselves. When you get down to actually producing a finely honed cover letter, you realize that you need to do more than merely recite your education and experiences. Indeed, you almost cannot record and report your qualifications without making certain representations and asking your reviewer to draw certain inferences. You want the hiring lawyer or manager who reviews your resume and other materials to recognize certain things about you. The data that you present is simply data, things like degrees and certificates earned, awards won, grade-point average and class standing, volunteer and pro bono experiences, and so on. Your challenge is to help the reviewer discern what that data says about your ability to perform their job in the near future. Your past accomplishments mean nothing to prospective employers unless those accomplishments reflect your character in ways that predict how you will perform a specific job for one or more of those prospective employers. You should therefore in this **Step 4** deliberately discern and articulate those attributes, characteristics, and skills that you wish employers to infer from your past education and experience.

Don't leave employers guessing. Tell them not just what you've done but also who you are and what you can do. Do not simply list what you've done. Instead, characterize, package, and present yourself as having certain characteristics, attributes, and skills that will get a prospective employer's job done.

Know Your Character and Skills

To put the same point another way, the strongest job candidates, those who are most likely to get the job that they desire, are the candidates who know who they are and can say so. Every job candidate has both strengths and weaknesses. The stronger candidates are not necessarily the ones with more of the strengths, greater strength where they have them, and fewer weaknesses. Rather, the stronger candidates are the ones who *know their strengths* and can share them quickly, concisely, and easily. Remember that information is among your primary obstacles to employment. You have so little time to get the right information to the right person so that the right employers consider you for employment. Average resume review time can be as short as five to seven seconds, spent mostly in checking your current and previous employment plus education. Beyond that data, you need to convey your strong points quickly, concisely, and powerfully, in any forum or format, whether on your written resume, in a cover letter, or in a brief reception-area introduction or brief elevator ride. Many other candidates may have gone to your undergraduate college or law school, or schools like them, graduating with similar honors. Several other candidates may have similar prior employment experience and even similar strong recommendation letters. How does your data uniquely reflect your special attributes, skills, character, and commitment? Whether or not your insights into your character actually appear on a resume, which in small respects they sometimes do, you should hope that you have at least a brief opportunity somewhere in the hiring process to articulate your strengths. Indeed, when you reach the interview stage, you should expect to do so. Know your strengths. Not to do so could be fatal to your preferred employment opportunities. Refer to this section whenever you feel undistinguished from other job candidates.

Discern Your Unique Qualities

So if you should in some sense *package* or *characterize* yourself, then how do you do so? Your key lies in projecting what your past education, employment, and experiences may do for your employer in the new employment that you seek. When you answer the classic interview question, "What do you see as your strength?" you should be helping the employer project you doing its job well. For example, if your education and experience prove you to be a strong administrator, able to address multiple tasks competently, timely, and consistently, and your desired job requires strong administrative skill, then prepare to say and show that you are a strong administrator. If instead your prior success proves you to be an outstanding communicator orally, in writing, or both, and your desired job requires strong communication skills, then prepare to say and show that you are a strong communicator. If in addition your job-search materials reflect that you master complex technical problems and fields quickly, and your desired job requires technical skill, then prepare to say and show that you readily acquire and use technical knowledge well. Notice that each of these examples of character and skill relates to a specific job function. You are not simply claiming that you are competent, masterful, resourceful, accomplished, creative, innovative, or trustworthy. You are not simply throwing around strong, positive adjectives to describe yourself and adverbs to describe your actions. You are instead relating strong, positive qualities to specific types of job functions like administration, communication, or acquisition and use of technical knowledge. A good recommendation letter actually does exactly that. Read carefully what your recommenders say about you. Use those insights to characterize your education and experience as reflecting your job character and skills.

Share Your Character and Skills

Of course, discerning your character, qualities, and skills is only the first step toward developing stronger job-search resources. Because you have hidden characteristics and attributes that employers would value if they only knew, you must also spend time in this **Step 4** not just writing about those attributes but also planning how to reveal them. Resumes and cover letters should reflect these projected characteristics, attributes, and skills. Resumes and cover letters can state that your education, awards, prior employment, or other experiences required that you administer complex programs, communicate effectively, problem solve in interdisciplinary teams, collaborate and coordinate with technical experts, or develop innovative systems and solutions, all things that prospective employers may highly value. Simply recording your place and dates of prior employment tells a prospective employer little. Instead, state how your employment benefited your prior employer. If your prior work reduced expenses, increased revenue, or solved systems problems in ways that increased efficiency, or if your education qualified you to do so, then have your resume say so. Focus on accomplishments over responsibilities. You should also prepare to share orally, not just in writing, these attributes and skills. Develop and practice a thirty-second elevator speech, indeed several of them each relating to a different attribute or skill. Find a family member or friend with whom to practice talking about your character and skills for high-value work. Most of us find it hard to boast. That reluctance is good until you are looking for a job, when liberally sharing your attributes and skill sets, if not outright boasting, is both wise and necessary. You must get over that reluctance. You must hone your skill at stating concisely and convincingly the actual attributes that your prior experience has shown that you possess and are ready to use for your prospective employer's benefit.

Show More Than Tell

One good way to get ready to demonstrate your character and expertise is to recall and rehearse one or more good stories that show how your accomplished something in your education or prior employment or experience. We respond to stories more than descriptions. Your stories, though, need a clear focus and purpose. Don't tell stories simply to be amusing. Instead, give an example of a challenging circumstance that you faced in prior employment, volunteer service, or another relevant setting. Then describe what you did in that circumstance and the positive difference that your actions made in the outcome. These issue-action-results stories prove your capability in ways that simply describing your duties cannot. These stories show you doing valuable things, proving your skill and character. Prospective employers and others who are ready to help you along the way to your preferred job remember those stories, when they forget the descriptions that you would otherwise give. Indeed, prospective employers know the value of situational interviewing in which they ask you to describe a time when you did something specific. You should be ready with the accounts and stories that will satisfy that approach. Develop a story for each of the job skills that your preferred future employers may require, whether those skills involve research, writing, advocacy, other communication, organization, consistency, problem solving, practice or business development, relationship management, file management, financial management, teamwork, or other common and highly valuable functions.

STEP 5:

Build Your Network

Why Networks Matter

In **Step 5**, you identify and record in your job-search journal all of your acquaintances who you believe may know a lawyer who could be quietly looking to hire another lawyer. Here again is why networks matter. As already indicated, employers often recruit by word of mouth for open positions that they have not posted. Lawyers and law firms are especially reluctant to post open positions for the whole world to see. You learn about these open positions only by communicating with those lawyers yourself or by hearing from other persons with whom they have shared their interest in hiring. Online searches and other reviews of job postings won't help you find these open positions for which no listing exists. You learn about these unlisted open positions only through private networks, not through published sources. Indeed, some employers post jobs simply to satisfy hiring protocols, at the same time fully expecting to recruit and hire instead only by word of mouth. Private networks are responsible for a large percentage of new hires, as much as 70% according to some sources, while online applications may account for as little as 15% of new hires. You may be four or five times as likely to get a job through networking as through applying online. Now do you see how important your network is?

Everyone Has a Network

You are not alone in your job search. You have a network, probably one that is significantly more extensive than you imagine. Many candidates get their job because of their network contacts. Job searching is not a do-it-alone activity. Finding and winning a job takes a village, a social and professional group surrounding and supporting you. To mix metaphors, you may feel like you are in your own corner, on your own island, or sailing solo in your job search. You are not. Everyone has a network. You have longstanding and deep relationships with some of your network contacts, particularly family members but also old friends like college roommates, sorority or fraternity members, and even high school classmates and hunting or fishing buddies. Many of those acquaintances will know lawyers, law firms, and other employers of lawyers. Other network contacts arising more recently out of your law studies make natural network contacts for job searching. Consider especially your law school classmates who may know of jobs in which they have no interest but would suit you. Include law professors and deans, adjunct professors who remain in law practice, and alumni mentors with whom you worked on a special volunteer or pro bono project. Other network contacts, like former co-workers in non-law fields, may seem unlikely to know lawyers but can still produce important job leads and information. Candidates sometime even get fruitful law-job leads from neighbors, family members of old friends, and even barbers and hairdressers who happen to know lawyers through their own service occupations. Yes, lawyers talk to their barbers and hairdressers. Refer to **Step 5** whenever you feel like you are alone in your job-search process. You are not alone.

58

List Network Contacts

The point in this **Step 5** is not to identify only the handful of your most-trusted placement professionals and career advisors. Rather, cast a broad net that includes anyone you know who may help you in one way or another with your job search, particularly with job leads. As suggested above, begin with family and friends, and then classmates, professors, and alumni from both your law school and undergraduate institution. Also include former co-workers and supervisors, volunteer leaders under whom you served, mentors, and any other individuals who you believe may know a lawyer who has a job opening or lead. When you record your network contacts, one by one, you have a longer list, probably much longer, than you expect. If you have a hard time generating your network-contacts list, then think first of formal associations or informal groups to which you belong, communities and circles within which you move, and organizations within which you have contacts. While contacts within legal communities like local litigators, prosecutors and defenders, transactional lawyers, and lawyers serving certain industries are best for generating law-job leads, think also of those communities that rely on lawyers such as law enforcement, social work, business, and government. And do not neglect social and recreational circles. You find plenty of professionals in running clubs, classic-car groups, sailing clubs, and other recreational and hobby groups.

Expand Your Network

Include in your **Step 5** network-contacts list new contacts that you plan to make with lawyers, judges, and persons who know lawyers who may be hiring in your preferred field in your preferred geographic area. Be both thoughtful of existing network contacts and effortful about creating new ones, telling new contacts what you want to do, where you want to do it, and why you are a qualified candidate for it. Especially if your network-contacts list seems inadequate to the task of creating job leads, then expand your network. Don't be embarrassed to pursue new network contacts. Professionals deliberately cultivate their networks for many reasons, job hunting only one reason among those many others. Networks also help professionals discover and attract new clients, learn about new methods and resources, create and sustain helpful referral networks for other expertise, meet new standards and regulations, and build a reputation for community engagement. When you have a need for expertise, don't you like to know people who know people? Be one of those resources. Then make your job search one part of your larger network equation. You need not make job search your only reason for reaching out to someone who may know by word of mouth of an open position. Bring some value of your own to the new network contact. Find something that may interest and be of value to the new network contact whom you wish to reach, such as a new law development. Use that helpful information to start your conversation with the new network contact. Make your inquiry about open positions only a part of the larger network relationship. Be a giver, not only a taker. When you do so, you have planted a seed that may grow into a relationship that will benefit both of you. Build your network through acquaintances of family members and friends, professional-organization events, alumni contacts, career fairs, and even cold calls (following networking etiquette) to lawyers and other professionals who know lawyers. Contact the authors of articles who have written recently in your field of interest, or leaders or members of affinity organizations of which you are a member or with which you hope to connect. Reach out creatively and thoughtfully to expand your network.

Employ Your Network

Simply by listing your network contacts, you should begin to find the ideas and energy for how your network can help you find and pursue job leads. You employ your network primarily through informational contacts, particularly informational interviews as explained in **Step 3**. Your first deliberate network contacts may produce actual job leads or referrals to go see other contacts who may know of leads. Your contacts with the persons whom you list may also produce their own offers to investigate on your behalf. As you list and contact your network, record what you learn from those contacts. If someone tells you that they will contact someone else for you, then make that note and, when the note reminds you later that you haven't heard, consider checking back with that network contact. Their inquiry may not have been successful, but in the meantime they may have had another idea or heard of something else. Remember to keep these contacts a two-way street. Think of how you can help them, even if your help is simply giving them the name of someone who might have been looking for their service. Referring a client to a lawyer is a good way for you to get the lawyer thinking of what the lawyer can do in return for you, such as give you a job lead.

Writing Thank-You Notes

You should write a thank-you note for every substantial network contact that you made, particularly for any informational interview. Thank-you notes have several purposes, all of them helpful to your job search. First, they demonstrate your thoughtfulness, thankfulness, and sensitivity. They prove that you have the kind of character that your interview suggested. Second, they remind the professional whom you interviewed of the fact of your meeting and the common purposes that the two of you shared. Your thank-you note may, for instance, supply a reference or link that the professional requested of you. Your note may also remind the professional that you look forward to receiving specific information that the professional offered to share. Third, the thank-you note projects forward your interest in maintaining the relationship. Your note can, for instance, refer to an upcoming professional gathering at which you might express your hope to see the professional again. Your note could even tip off the professional to a valuable upcoming opportunity, whether a professional-networking or professional-education event, or even a social event other networking professionals are likely to attend. Finally, your thank-you note can and should confirm your contact information, enclosing your business card. The professional may have had more to share with you after you met but may have forgotten how to reach you. Your thank-you note confirms your contact information, even if you supplied it when you met. Your thank-you note may be an email, although emails do not carry the personal touch, thoughtfulness, and earnestness of ordinary mail. You may use word processing and business stationery and envelopes for a thank-you note, but consider purchasing specific thank-you cards that you can handwrite with an enclosed business card. If you do buy special cards, then make them professional in appearance, not offhand or trite. Monographed cards are old fashioned but can impress. Whatever you do, do not underestimate the significance of a thank-you note. Highly placed professionals will routinely tell you that they expect and appreciate thank-you notes. Write a thank-you note even when the professional with whom you met didn't open, and may have closed, doors through which you had hoped to walk. Some professionals even report turning back for hiring to a candidate whom they rejected, on the basis in part of a thank-you note.

Other Network Etiquette

The prior section on thank-you notes should alert you to the significance of network etiquette. You have two reasons to show especially good manners and decorum in making any network contact. First, professionals comprise most of your network, you hope *esteemed* professionals. They already conduct themselves following professional conventions and protocols. They likely dress professionally, speak articulately and circumspectly, and generally expect other professionals with whom they interact to likewise do so. Second, when you network, you are asking those esteemed professionals to share their time. They are unlikely to do so unless you act with appropriate gratitude and decorum. So, act professionally with your network contacts, even if they happen to relax and be more conversational and informal than you usually see them or other professionals act. Dress professionally, be on time, and introduce yourself professionally with your full name and status such as that you are a graduating student at a certain law school. Don't waste time unduly with useless small talk. Prepare for the contact, both researching your contact's background and planning specific job-search questions that you intend to ask. Have both your thirty-second elevator speech and your two-minute story ready to share with the contact. Thirty seconds or two minutes may be all that you get. Be friendly, positive, and engaging, not low energy, negative, and depressing. In a long and busy day, your contact may appreciate a moment's boost of positive and refreshing energy. Do not initiate a network contact unless you have a relatively specific outcome that you can articulate that is helpful to your job search. And make the contact beneficial reciprocally if you possibly can. Bring something to the proverbial table, even if it seems to you to be modest, such as sharing another network contact's name as someone whom the contact with whom you meet might share an interest.

Email Etiquette

Take a moment here to review your email etiquette. While email is very efficient and common for professional communications, its efficiency and informality invites etiquette breaches. You should be using email to network, make initial employer contacts, respond to job postings that require or invite electronic submission, and thank others for help with your job search. Do not use email to apply for positions where the posting does not specifically invite email submissions. Use regular mail instead in those instances. Do not use email as the only way that you acknowledge and thank your interviewers or others who have helped you substantially with your job search. Always treat email as you would a letter, with the same deliberation, respectful tone, and proofreading. Always use a descriptive subject line. Never send email from an inappropriately personal email address or from your current employer's address. Instead, use your law school account or your personal account with an appropriate address (name and numbers, not descriptors). Treat email as non-confidential. You don't know who may read it. Do not send mass emails. Place job-search emails in appropriately marked electronic folders for saving. No emoticons, color fonts, all-caps text, or abbreviations. Reply to email promptly, the same day or within no less than 24 hours.

A Recording System

If you wish, then you can make your **Step 5** network-contacts list a long narrative in your electronic job-search file. For better organization, you may instead choose to insert in **Step 5** a three-column table of network contacts. Record the contact name in the first column, making your record alphabetical so that you can easily locate a name. Record the contact date and content (what you learned) in the second column. Use the third column to project the follow up that you should take with that contact. Keeping the table up to date day to day will remind you of whom you have contacted, whom you need to contact, and with whom you need to follow up. In a way, your contact list is the heart of your job search. Each step preliminary to your contact list is just another good intention or idea. Your contact list turns intentions and ideas into real opportunities for action. To get a job, you must reach out to employers. Reaching out to network contacts is your first real step toward reaching employers. Some of your network contacts may actually be looking to hire. Indeed, some of them may not yet be looking to hire but may consider hiring when they learn that you are looking. In other words, your network contacts may help you brainstorm new opportunities, not just identify existing ones. Indeed, when you have found your job, you may decide to keep your network-contacts list up to date for its other benefits, like attracting and referring clients. Just keeping your name and expertise in the mind of others can help generate new work while simultaneously serving those others. You do both yourself and your contacts a service by staying in touch. Be known, and be of service.

STEP 6:

Discover Job Openings

Discovering Job Openings Matters

Here then is one of your most-important steps toward getting that great job: discovering and compiling actual job openings that could potentially be your first or next lawyer job. In **Step 6**, you should record in your electronic job-search journal every job opening that you discover and for which you qualify or may qualify, and may have some interest in applying. This section should be one of the largest sections of your job-search journal. While researching your job market, confirming your network, and working on the other steps in this job-search program, you should also be discovering specific available jobs for which you would consider applying. When you do identify job openings for which you may qualify and that you may pursue, list those job openings here in **Step 6**. You are going to apply for some of these jobs. That step is coming. But for now, record these job openings so that you can see the specific opportunities that exist for you. See these job openings as your leads, those critical bits of information one of which is going to lead you to your job. With diligent searching, your job-openings list will grow. Seeing your list grow will encourage you further in all steps of your job search. We tend to forget much of what we once knew. Within a week or two of learning about several job openings, you will have forgotten about at least some of them. Listing them reminds you that they are

66

now or once were open, spurring you on to further critical action. Also list how and where you discovered the job openings so that you can increase those activities to learn about other jobs. If you cannot regularly add to your **Step 5** list, then you need to refocus your job search to produce more job-opening leads.

Dig for Job Postings

Refer to **Step 5** and plan more time and activities digging for job leads whenever you realize that you are making too little real progress. Pound the pavement, even if only virtual pavement. Dig for job leads. Use both general and lawyer-only lists, national, statewide, and local lists, and affinity lists, as further explained below. Just because no position appears in one list doesn't mean that a position won't appear in another. Employers generally control where their jobs post. Some employers routinely post to several lists all at once. Other employers post to only one or two lists. Some employers first post to one or two lists and then post to additional lists if they don't get the candidates that they want. Employers are also constantly posting, modifying posts, removing posts, and posting again, for the same, different, or redesigned positions, as the employer makes and withdraws, and as candidates accept or reject, positions, and the employer learns more about the labor market. Keep reviewing the same and different online job lists. Just because you reviewed a certain list last week or last month doesn't mean that you shouldn't review that same list again. Chances are good that new positions will appear. After all, in theory given the relatively short timetable on which employers tend to hire, within a few weeks every posted position should have changed.

National Job Lists

You have many ways to investigate and discover job openings. An obvious place, one to which the above **Step 3** on evaluating your job market already referred, is in online job listings. The professional networking site LinkedIn is a primary example of a national site that includes national job listings. Specific national online job-list services like CareerBuilder, ZipRecruiter, Monster, USAJobs, Glassdoor, Jobs2Careers, and Snagajob are general sources that include lawyer openings. ZipRecruiter and other national lists compile and organize job listings from many other online sources. Other services like Lawjobs.com, Lawmatch, BCG Attorney Search, and Barrettgrouplegal list job postings only for lawyers. Don't stop, though, at reviewing national lists compiled by job recruiters. Lawyers associate in national organizations for general professional purposes, such as in the American Bar Association, National Bar Association, American Association for Justice (formerly known as the American Trial Lawyers Association), Defense Research Institute (for insurance defense lawyers), and Association of Corporate Counsel (for in-house lawyers). Some of these organizations post job listings as a service to their members. Some also offer discount or free membership to law students, granting student access to job lists. These national associations also hold frequent conferences at which their lawyer members gather to network. The associations often encourage law student attendance, sometimes even providing scholarships for conference costs. Lawyers attending national conferences will often treat attending law students with special respect, recognizing the commitment that those students have made to the lawyer's specialty field. Attend a national conference of lawyers with your portfolio, networking effectively, and job leads and offers are distinct possibilities in those favored settings.

State and Local Job Lists

State and local bar associations may also post job listings including postings that do not reach national online sites. State bars often list jobs online or in other member forums including specialty sections. Once you decide the state in which you intend to license, check these statewide job listings for opportunities in your geographic area and field of interest. If you intend to practice law in a certain county large enough to sustain its own local bar association, then chances are good that the local bar association also posts local job listings, some of which may not appear on national or statewide online sites. Beyond these general statewide and local bar associations, lawyers associating at the state level often also do so through practice area or specialty field, such as the Prosecuting Attorneys Association, Criminal Defense Attorneys, or Trial Lawyers Association of the state. Once again, these associations often list job postings. Some, such as the statewide prosecutors' associations, may even serve as a collection point for job applications for local job opportunities. Be sure to include state and local bar associations and specialty associations in your search for job postings.

Affinity Job Lists

Lawyers also form associations around a variety of affinities including ethnicity or ancestry, gender, and even recreational interests. Black lawyers associate nationally as the National Bar Association and also the National Conference of Black Lawyers, and statewide and locally in associated chapters or separate organizations. The Irish-American Bar Association and other ancestry-based associations also have statewide and local chapters, like the Polish-American Legal Society in the Detroit area, some of which provide local job listings. The Women Lawyers Association has many local chapters, some of which provide job listings and other job-search services. Lawyers also organize across affinity and gender at national, statewide, and local levels, as in the Black Women Lawyers Association of Michigan and Black Women Lawyers Association of Chicago, again at times offering job listings. Law firms have increasing reason to recruit diverse candidate pools, meaning that they are more likely than previously to post job listings with affinity organizations whose communications reach minority communities. Lawyers also associate through the Lawyers & Judges Golf Association, Volunteer Lawyers for the Arts, and other associations of lawyers interested in recreational, cultural, and social interests. Explore these associations for job postings particularly if you share the association's interest or affinity.

Your Network Job Leads

As already addressed in the prior **Step 5,** online job postings are not your only source for job leads, indeed possibly not even your primary source. Your job-search network may be better at producing specific job leads in your geographic area and within your qualifications and interests. Remember too that the job leads that your network produces may be for opportunities that the employer does not intend to post. You may thus not be competing with dozens of other applicants when you learn of a job lead through your network contacts. List these leads in **Step 6** just as you list leads that you discover from job postings online. Highlight and investigate these network-generated job leads. Treat them with priority value compared to the postings that you discover online. Ensure that you are generating job leads through your network. If you are not, then you may not be asking the right questions of the right network contacts, or not making the right reciprocal approaches in which you offer your contact some value, or not sharing the right resources that communicate your skill. This step of generating and listing job leads out of your job-search network may be your most critical activity, that one step the effectiveness of which will determine the speed and satisfaction of your job search. Don't let this step be your Achilles heel. Here is a valuable tip that placement professionals sometimes share: you may network more successfully for job leads by communicating with the lawyers who are actually doing the work with which you want to help rather than with the firm's managers and human-resources specialists. The lawyers doing the work may already be recruiting the expertise that they need, lining up the inside-track candidates, long before the managers and human-resources specialists are posting or otherwise sharing the job opportunity. Be sure to network with the lawyers who do the work, not just with the lawyers or managers who hire those who do the work.

Specialty Field Job Lists

Lawyers also organize nationally around specialty fields. You will find national lawyer specialty-field associations as diverse as the American Agricultural Law Association, American Intellectual Property Law Association, American Academy of Matrimonial Lawyers, American College of Real Estate Lawyers, Alliance of Business Lawyers, Association of Business Trial Lawyers, Transportation Lawyers Association, National Association of Consumer Bankruptcy Attorneys, International Association of Entertainment Lawyers, and Sports Lawyers Association, and dozens more. The American Bar Association also has many national sections around specialty fields, serving as national associations of lawyers practicing in those fields. Many of these national associations of lawyers organized around fields encourage law students to join for free or at discounts. Many also list job opportunities. Even those that don't list job opportunities are likely to hold conferences at which networking for job leads is possible. Beyond the lawyer specialty associations, you may find attractive law or law-related job postings in trade papers, magazines, and journals. Business associations, industry associations, and other professional associations may post in-house counsel, compliance counsel, labor counsel, tax counsel, contract counsel, corporate or governance counsel, risk management, and other lawyer positions for specific non-law-firm employers. The same trade journals may also post law-related, law-degree-preferred positions in human resources, labor negotiations, employee benefits, or other administrative fields in which you may have relevant qualifications and also have an interest.

Job Fairs

Law students and lawyers also discover job openings through national and regional job fairs. A job fair brings multiple national, regional, or local employers to a single location to meet job candidates. While you may associate job fairs only with undergraduate programs, employers of lawyers also participate in job fairs. Some of those job fairs focus broadly on law or law-related jobs, like the American Bar Association Law Student Division Career Fair and the Boston Lawyers Group Job Fair. Other fairs recruit for specific fields of law, such as the Health Law Student Conference and Job Fair, the Loyola Patent Law Interview Program, and the Annual Prosecutorial Opportunities Symposium. Other fairs recruit minority lawyers, such as the Hispanic National Bar Association Job Fair and Conference, Rocky Mountain Diversity Legal Career Fair, IMPACT Career Fair for Law Students and Attorneys with Disabilities, and Northwest Minority Job Fair. Still other fairs recruit across field and affinity, such as the National Black Prosecutors Association Job Fair. Investigate which job fairs have employers attending with whom you would like to interview. Job fairs typically require registration with cost, but register early for the right job fairs, looking for scholarships to defray registration cost. Job fairs also typically require you to bid for interviews with specific employers who will rely for interview offer on your resume. Once again, investigate each job fair's requirements, and ensure that you present a sound resume reviewed by your law school's career officer. See **Step 7** below for how to prepare for an interview. In brief, wear professional attire, arrive early, prepare thoroughly as you would for any other interview, and be positive no matter how brief the interview and distracting the circumstances. Follow up with thank-you letters, just as you would for any other interview. Again, see **Step 7** on interview conduct.

Solo Practitioners

Even if you plan to enter practice alone, starting your own firm, you may benefit from exploring job postings and recording and pursuing job leads. When lawyers and law firms advertise positions for hire, they are indicating that they have a surplus of work. Lawyers meet work demands, though, not merely by hiring new lawyers. Lawyers also meet work demands by referring matters to lawyers in other firms, co-counseling with lawyers from other firms on matters, and contracting out parts of matters to other lawyers doing contract-service work. Every new hire carries certain risks about which law firms are well aware. Those risks include that the new lawyer will not be a good fit, not have the expected skills, not quickly learn the firm's systems and expectations, or simply not like the work. Hires are commitments, often not easily undone. By contrast, referring, co-counseling, or contracting out matters carries fewer or at least different risks that a firm may prefer to incur over the risks of a new hire. If you want to build a solo practice, then you might consider contacting some of those lawyers who have indicated interest in hiring and firms that have posted open positions to see whether you might take on some of that extra work in your solo practice. You might also get an attractive job offer that you cannot and should not resist. Solo practice has its benefits, but so does practice with one or more other lawyers. Solo practitioners can do well to know who's hiring because hiring recruitment routinely indicates an excess of available work.

STEP 7:

Apply, Apply, Apply

Your Job Applications Matter

Actually applying for a job in this **Step 7** is distinct from learning about the job opportunity and listing it in **Step 6.** Keeping separate lists of opportunities discovered (**Step 6**) and opportunities for which you have applied (**Step 7**) is important. Just because you learn about a job doesn't mean that you should or will apply for it. Yet you need a comprehensive and growing list of job opportunities out of which to select jobs for which to apply. This one-two punch is why you should think of investigating, discovering, and recording job leads as one step and then applying for specific jobs as a separate step. Both steps are critical to your job-search success. You are unlikely to get a job if you don't know what jobs are out there for you, which **Step 6** addresses. You are just as unlikely to get a job if you don't apply for the jobs that you know are out there for you, which **Step 7** addresses. You should think of the **Step 7** application process as distinct from the **Step 6** discovering-openings process for another reason. The application process is a world unto itself. A successful application takes any number of deft moves from the timing and routing of the application to the materials that you include, the follow up that you make, your interview, your follow up to the interview, and your response to the job offer.

Discovering a job opening doesn't mean that the job is yours. The job is instead yours only when you successfully navigate a subtle process that the employer has designed specifically to discern how good you are at such navigation. Employers don't make the application process easy because the work for which they will employ you isn't easy without the skills to navigate it.

How to Apply

Some, and perhaps most or all, of your job applications will require completing a job-application form at some point in the process. Employers use job-application forms to winnow qualified from unqualified, and preferred from less-desired, candidates. You should therefore put your proverbial best foot forward, including on the job-application form all of your priority qualifications that the form permits or requires. Do not, in other words, treat the form perfunctorily, even if you are submitting a cover letter and resume that highlight your significant accomplishments, and even if you know one or more lawyers at the employer's location who know you and your qualifications. Some reviewers may see only your job application and not your resume. Importantly, employers also use job-application forms to communicate your rights, such as equal-employment opportunity, *and the employer's rights*, such as to terminate you at any time that the employer discovers that your job-application information is inaccurate. You should therefore ensure that your job application is entirely accurate. Fairly or not, employers also draw impressions from how candidates complete or don't complete job applications properly, clearly, comprehensively, and succinctly. Treat your job applications as you would the preparation of your cover letter or resume, with the same care and presentation. Follow directions. Use black ink and legible writing if handwritten, and a common business-style font if typewritten. Use correct grammar, spelling, and punctuation. Answer every question that you can answer even if the answer is in your resume. Do not give *see-resume* answers. If a question does not apply, then write or type *not applicable*. The employer may construe a blank answer, such as whether you have had any felony convictions for crime involving dishonesty or violence, as your effort to conceal negative information. Your desired or required compensation level is one question that some employers ask but that you may properly avoid answering directly. Writing *negotiable* is a common and fair response. Your desired start date is another question to which you may fairly reply *open* rather than give a specific response.

Record Your Job Applications

The gist of **Step 7** is that you record each job application that you make, here in this section of your online job-search journal, along with the progress of that application and your discernment about what next steps to take with each application. Again, winning a job is not as simple as applying. Indeed, a successful application doesn't win you the job. A successful application simply advances you to the next step of the application process toward winning you that job. These multiple steps are why you need a place in **Step 7** of your online job-search journal to record carefully, diligently, and accurately the status of each job-application process, from submission to response, invitation to interview, interview follow up, request for references, offer, response to offer, and acceptance. If you don't have a single instantly accessible place to record your job-application process, then you are more likely to make one or more missteps in one or more application processes, where a single misstep can disqualify you for the job. If you applied for only one job and advanced through only that one job-application process, then you would likely have in mind at all time precisely where you were in the process and what you would like to see happen next. Your job search very likely won't be that simple. You will probably apply for several or even many jobs, and you may well advance at different times to different stages of different processes in some of those applications. Keep track here in **Step 7** of each of those application processes.

Your Approach to Job Applications

To catch a fish, you must have lines in the water. Make sure that you are submitting job applications. Prospective employers must know that you are available if they are going to interview and hire you. Do not overlook the significance of making actual applications. Get your application materials together, and then pull the trigger. Apply, apply, and apply. The habit, discipline, and practice of making applications can encourage you to take other important steps, energizing your job search. Your failure to actually apply can stultify, discourage, and frustrate your other fruitful actions. Also, do not delay applications. Just because a job listing remains open does not mean that the employer is still waiting for a qualified candidate. During your delay, the employer may already have interviewed multiple other candidates and even selected the lone candidate for hire. Employers sometimes leave job postings up while completing an already nearly finished hiring process, such as while waiting for reference and background checks to confirm the selected candidate's qualifications. Do not collect, hold, and relish **Step 6** job openings without executing on them in this application **Step 7**. Refer to this section frequently to be sure that you have several lines in the water at once. Fish only bite when the bait is in the water. Keep baited lines in the water. You never know when the big fish is circling the hook. Apply with that disciplined and energized sense of anticipation and excitement.

Job-Application Contents

The means through which you apply for each job should dictate in part your application's contents. Follow all instructions that the application process supplies. If, for instance, you apply online, and the online forum instructs that you submit resume only without including letters of recommendation or writing

77

sample, then do not append those additional materials that the instructions prohibit. You will only be proving that you don't know how to follow instructions. If, for another example, the application process instructs to submit as an email attachment a resume with two recommendation letters, all in pdf file format, then submit only those three documents in precisely that file required file format. Again, if you do anything else, then you will only be proving that you don't know how to satisfy the employer's processes. If you can't even apply for the job properly, then how would you possibly perform it properly if the employer hired you for it? Follow instructions. On the other hand, if the application process does not clearly specify your application's contents, then you should put your proverbial best foot forward. If, for instance, you apply in person by delivering your application materials to the network contact who invited your application, and that contact gave you no specific instruction, then you should in all likelihood supply your most-articulate cover letter, best-looking resume, most-appropriate writing sample, and a couple of great recommendation letters, all fitted to the specific job opportunity if possible and appropriate. Don't skimp by supplying only a resume while waiting for the employer to invite your more-comprehensive and best job-search resources. Give the best that you've got at the first opportunity, especially when you have any reason to believe that your first application may be your only chance at getting the employer's attention. If on the other hand you *know* when you first apply that you will *definitely* get a follow-up interview, then you may wish to hold a writing sample, portfolio of written work products, premier recommendation letter, or other special job-search resource to share at the interview stage. Holding a trump card for the last trick can work but only if you know that you are still in the game.

Interviews

Interviews are a large subject unto themselves, one that some advisors would not even treat as part of the application process but instead as an independent special event. First consider the interview as part of the application process. To get a job, you are almost surely going to first need to meet in person the people who will hire you, and perhaps also those who will train and supervise you on the job, and maybe even some of your key co-workers. Hiring very often happens based on the face-to-face meetings, not merely the materials that you submit. Sometimes, probably rarely, the in-person interview can be relatively pro forma, almost an afterthought because of your superb and unique qualifications for a particular job for which few or no other candidates apply. Those instances, though, would be the exception, as you can imagine. Think then about why employers feel that these in-person encounters are necessary before extending an offer. Work relationships are some of the most significant relationships that any of us have. Many employees spend more time with one another than they do their own family members including spouse and children. Interviews can be tests of special knowledge, skill, and expertise. Just as often or more often, they are tests of your personality, demeanor, and social grace. When you learn the good news in the application process that the employer selected you for interview, you should listen carefully and, if necessary, gently inquire as to the nature of the interview. Many employers, particularly the interview manager or guide, will be quite open in advance as to the employer's purposes for the interview, whether purely an opportunity for key personnel to see how you get along with them or instead whether to evaluate your knowledge and skill.

Relational Interviews

Interviews come in several forms. The two primary forms are relational interviews and substantive interviews. The relational interview is at once both the easiest and the hardest interview format. The easy part is that you need not demonstrate special knowledge and expertise. You don't face any particular technical test other than to display the communication and relationship skills that the employer's representatives expect and accept. The employer's objective in a relational interview is that your interaction with your interviewers satisfies those interviewers that you can become a trusted member of a cohesive team. The team may include superiors, peers, and subordinates, toward each of whom you must show due respect. Be sure to engage each member of the interview team, even if some do not engage you. You must be deferential to superiors, respectful of peers, and especially respectful of subordinates although at the same time without subordinating yourself. Because many professionals exercise these interpersonal skills continuously, competently, and intuitively, *just being yourself* can be a reliable mantra, as long as you are naturally cordial, appropriate, thoughtful, sensitive, discrete, kind, warm, engaging, and respectful, which of course most of us are not, at least not all of the time. The point is that you must be not on your ordinary behavior but on your *best* behavior, and not for most of the interview but for *all* of the interview *and* for every greeting, introduction, informal chat, and parting comment that surrounds the interview. The employer is observing and evaluating you at every moment, indeed particularly in your unguarded moments. In relational interviews, some employers will deliberately design interactions meant to test your ability to maintain sound relations even when the interviewers subtly invite you not to do so. Resist gossip, disrespect, off-color comments, and any other unprofessional or indiscrete interaction even when, indeed especially when, invited to share in it. The employer is testing you. The test is not how willing you are to subvert professional norms but how able you are to recognize and maintain them even when others fail to do so. In relational interviews, smile and engage, be your warm and interested self, but don't let down your decorum guard until you are on your way home alone.

Substantive Interviews

The substantive interview is one in which the employer's objective is to test the veracity of the qualifications that your resume and other job-search resources represent that you possess. The substantive interview isn't simply showing you around the office, letting you spend ten to twenty minutes chatting informally with key personnel and then perhaps lunching socially with your core team, as in the case of a relational interview. Instead, in substantive interviews, the interview team will have prepared questions or discussion subjects in advance, expecting that you will respond in ways that prove that you have the knowledge, insight, and expertise that the job you seek will demand. The technical substance may be doctrinal, whether you know certain laws, rules, and regulations relating closely to the job. The technical substance may also be procedural, whether you know key processes, means, or methods for completing certain key job tasks. You can thus imagine that you would want some notice from your interview manager or guide of the interview's likely format and subjects to prepare as much as you can. Listen carefully to any such advice. If your interview manager offers none, then a polite inquiry as to whether you should expect specific technical questions or tests may be fair, particularly if you can do so without sounding as if you lack confidence in your qualifications. A helpful interview manager may give you helpful tips that certain interviewers have certain technical interests such as that one interviewer does municipal-bond financing work or that another writes and examines proxy statements. A tip of that kind would give you an opportunity to confirm that you at least know basically what that work means so that you are not caught entirely flat-footed when your interviewer attempts to engage you around your interviewer's favorite technical subject. A little knowledge can go a long way in a brief interview.

Second Interviews

You may of course have more than one round of interviews. A second round some time, often days but sometimes a few weeks, after the first round would generally mean that you have the core support within the organization that you need for hire. First-round interviews are often by the employees with whom you would most closely work if hired. Second-round interviews mean that you don't yet have the support of others in the employer's organization who could veto your hiring. Those others may include the firm's management-committee members, practice-group chairs, or other influential employees who, while not likely to work closely with you, wish to ensure that the organization continues to hire new employees who represent the organization's commitments and values. For that reason, second-round interviews are every bit as important as first-round interviews. Second-round interviews, though, are not generally relational or substantive. The employees who interviewed in the first round would already have confirmed your ability to relate well and any questions about your substantive expertise. Second-round interviews by higher-ups in the organization instead often address your understanding of and commitment to the organization's culture, mission, and values. Second-round interviews are not a matter of being first nice and then smart, as you would hope to be in first-round interviews. Instead, you must show your eagerness to behave and do as the organization's leaders generally expect. Those commitments may be to things like hard work, long hours, and large billings, or community involvement and service work, or client development (rainmaking), or your own continued professional development to acquire necessary special expertise. Researching the employer can give you helpful clues as to the commitments that you should, if willing, be prepared to reflect. At the same time, though, leaders within an organization can differ widely on their views of these things. Your second-round success may have more to do with your ability to read and respond to individual influential interviewers than to anything that you can learn and prepare for in advance.

Remote Interviews

One or more of your interviews may not be in person but instead accomplished remotely, by videoconference or even teleconference. More professionals are working remotely, and more professionals are communicating remotely with greater ease, comfort, and confidence. More employers are also conducting at least screening job interviews, even if not final interviews for the job, using videoconferencing systems. You may even have an interview in which some interviewers are in the room with you but others observing and communicating remotely. If you have no skill or experience at communicating using desktop or other videoconferencing systems, then your remote interview may go poorly and fail to reflect your true communication skill. Don't let your interview be the first time that you videoconference. Instead, practice, even if only using your own laptop or desktop computer camera or one supplied by your law school's career office. Indeed, even if your interview is in person rather than remote, consider working with your law school's career office to practice an interview using the computer's camera to record the interview as if it were remote. Then review the recording with your career advisor to evaluate your interview demeanor. One look can quickly show you small but distracting things that you can easily correct, whether saying *um*, rubbing your hands or clothing, looking down and away rather than making appropriate eye contact, or the opposite staring at your interviewer in uncomfortable manner. You may also pick up grooming and professional-dress issues, such as hair that you need to trim or that your suit needs tailoring or pressing.

Video Interviews

Whether or not you get to practice a video interview in advance of the real thing, consider the following appearance and etiquette issues. While you should wear the traditional business attire that you would wear to any interview, be sure in a video interview to avoid wearing patterns and stripes that might distort the video image. Also avoid high-gloss lipstick and makeup and prominent shiny jewelry that might reflect light back into the camera, distracting the interviewer. Speaking to a camera can be awkward at first. Focus instead on the interviewer's video image, speaking to the person as you would in any conversation. If the system locates the camera above or away from the interviewer's video image, then make frequent eye contact through the camera itself so that the interviewer can see your expression and attention naturally, as if you were face to face. Avoid excessive movement, especially distracting hand motions, but don't on the other hand be unusually stiff. Cameras capture body language, so let your enthusiasm and positive, relaxed energy show. Sit up and lean in attentively when the interviewer speaks, and use natural voice and facial expressions when speaking, especially smiles. Don't raise your voice unnaturally just because on remote camera. The microphone should capture your voice at natural volume. You or the technician can adjust it if not. Introduce yourself as you would in person, minus the handshake. Have paper and pen handy to jot very brief notes, especially the names of all interviewers. Use those names kindly and appropriately. Don't speak over the interviewer. Allow a moment's pause before answering. When you finish an answer, make your conclusion clear so that the interviewer knows that the interviewer can resume with the next question. Be aware of time so that you can conclude as you would any other interview, expressing interest in the job and thanking the interviewer. When the interview is over, say nothing about the interview until you have left the room. Open microphones may catch private comments.

Interview Research

Preparing for your interview is a key to your interview success. You first need to know as much as you can learn about both the job and your prospective employer, including (if you can) the persons interviewing you. Read carefully any information about the job that the employer has made publicly available, particularly the detailed job description if available. If you feel that the public information about the job is insufficient, and if you have a diplomatic way to learn more, such as a reference inside the organization or the contact information for the human-resource manager posting the position, then use that contact to request additional information about the job to help you prepare for your interview. The person who notified you of the interview request would be another appropriate contact from whom to request additional information. You may ask who will conduct the interview and what information about the firm that person can provide, although without pressing for answers. The employer may have disclosed all that they have or wish to disclose. Beyond knowing the job's details for your interview, you should also learn what you can about the employer. If the employer is a law firm, then study the firm's published mission and management philosophy, and its practice divisions or groups, the fields in which it concentrates its services, and the clients whom it serves. Learn what you can about its structure, such as the number of partners versus associates, the type of partners (equity and non-equity), the type of associates (partner track or non-partner track, permanent or contract), and the corporate form (partnership, limited partnership, professional limited-liability company). Know its office locations, how many lawyers are in each office, and what those lawyers do. If you know or can learn your interviewers' identities, then research their title and responsibility with the firm or other employer and also their backgrounds including law school and undergraduate institution, practice field, community service, and honors and awards. Much of this information will be on the employer's website, particularly if the employer is a law firm. You may glean other information about the firm and your interviewers from your network contacts, although be circumspect in asking around. Research is one thing but snooping another.

Interview Dress for Men

Your physical appearance can make a difference at an interview. As when meeting your future in-laws, you should want to look your best. For lawyer employment, business attire, as you would dress if going to court or a major business transaction, not business casual, is standard interview dress. Wear business attire even if you expect your interviewers to wear business casual, unless your interviewers instruct you not to wear business attire. For men, that means a black, dark gray, or navy blue wool or wool-blend single-breasted suit with plain buttons and without pocket square (pocket kerchief) or other adornment. Wear a white, long-sleeved dress shirt and white short-sleeved undershirt. Do not go without an undershirt (you may sweat from interview stress more than you expect), and do not wear a colored, patterned, or sleeveless undershirt. Choose a color-coordinated simple-patterned tie, not a bow-tie. Knot the tie at a length to your black belt, not above or below or below the belt. Ensure that the front of the tie is somewhat longer than the back of the tie and that you have tucked the back of the tie in its cloth loop so that the back of the tie does not stick out askew. Avoid cuff links and tie clip or pin, and rings in the ears, nose, eyebrow, tongue, lip, or any visible place else. Wear polished black shoes and over-calf solid black or dark-blue socks matching your suit. Avoid jewelry of any kind other than a modest ring and watch. Have a recent haircut, groomed hair, fresh shave, and groomed fingernails but no cologne. Carry an extra copy of your resume, cover letter, writing sample, and recommendation letters in a black or natural-colored leather folder or small briefcase.

Interview Dress for Women

The conventions for interview wear are similar for women as for men, starting with the admonition to wear business attire unless specifically instructed not to do so. Do not feel overdressed if your interviewers wear business casual while you are in your best business suit. Interviewers expect candidates to dress more formally.   For women, your suit should ordinarily be skirted rather than pants, not trendy but traditional, conservative cut. Wear pants suit only if you don't wear skirts.   A conservative dress with a quality-fabric jacket can be an acceptable alternative. If you wear a skirt or dress, then the length should be at least to the knee and the cut straight or with only slight flare. If the skirt has a slit, then the slit should be short, especially if the skirt is only to your knee and not below. Suit color should be black, navy, or gray. Your blouse should be solid white or subtle color. Wear low-heeled, closed-toe, polished pumps over skin-tone hose. Shoe color may be black, navy, or dark brown.   Style hair to professional image. Pull hair back if long and in the face. Keep makeup subdued and well blended. No lipstick on the teeth. No more than one earring per ear, and no or only very light perfume. As for men, carry an extra copy of your resume, cover letter, writing sample, and recommendation letters in a black or natural-colored leather folder or small briefcase. Carrying both a purse and folder or briefcase can be awkward, so carry a purse, dark-colored leather, only if you must.

Interview Preparation

In addition to researching about the job and employer to prepare for your interviewers, you also need to prepare yourself for the interview.   You should, for instance, leave your interviewers with the clear impression that you knew your employment goals, had strong communication skills, were confident in what you could do, were interested in the job, were committed to the employer's mission, had specific examples of your accomplishments, and helped your interviewers understand who you are. To accomplish those objectives, you need to prepare articulate statements about yourself that you can make with or without your interviewers prompting.   Indeed, one good statement to rehearse is what you would say given a substantial lull in the conversation. Have two or three subjects to broach in any such lull that would lead your interviewers back to something positive about your qualifications. You should also have a two- or three-minute speech ready to comply with the interviewer's directive to tell the interviewer about yourself. Rehearse that opening until you are fully satisfied with its content, impressed with its articulateness, and comfortable with your delivery. You only get one chance to make a first impression. Make it chronological, from the oldest important detail to the newest, leaving your interviewer where you stand today. Include one mention of your upbringing and then your education, work experience, job and career goal, and the value that you would provide to the firm. Have prepared, rehearsed, and effective answers to why you want the job for which you are applying, what qualifies you for that job, and what are your strengths and weaknesses. If asked, then do share a weakness. To claim that you have none is to suggest that you are disinterested in your further professional development. Also be ready to give an example of where that weakness showed up. But when you share your weakness, though, also share how you are remediating it. Don't be surprised if the interviewer asks you what you know about the employer. Have a positive answer that shows that you did your research, but also consider asking the interviewer for more information about the employer, particularly if you were unable to discern substantial information. Show knowledge, but also show interest. Also be ready to answer the question of where you see yourself in five or ten years. Unless the position for which you are applying is clearly temporary, do not project yourself as working somewhere other than the employer's workplace.

Demonstrative Answers

Employers properly believe that your performance with them is likely to approximate your prior performance with others. We don't change overnight, just because we have a new job. To learn from you what you have already done that you may repeat effectively for your prospective employer, interviewers may often ask you to describe a time when you demonstrated a certain skill.

Those skills may include managing projects, managing people, dealing with conflict, dealing with change, providing sound service, innovating or creating, motivating yourself and others, working as part of an effective team, communicating orally, communicating in writing, learning new technology, developing new uses for technology, leadership, planning, and even delegating and working with subordinate staff effectively. Think of examples for these and other skills, and be ready to share those examples. Doing so should increase your confidence about the interview. Even if your interviewers do not ask these past-performance questions, then volunteer your answers to them anyway to give your interviewers the same specific insight and encouragement that you are already a valuable professional. If you didn't anticipate the precise past-performance question that your interviewer actually asks, and you can't think of an answer on the spot, then you may be able to use your prepared examples of how you handled a similar situation. The job description should help you anticipate performance-based questions. Go through the job description, thinking of examples when you performed each of its requirements effectively in another setting. If the interviewer's specific question stumps you, then use one of those examples instead, referring to the job description. Your best overarching strategy in interview is to prove your value to the employer. Demonstrative answers do so. Prepare for them.

Negative Experiences

Don't stumble over interview questions that ask you to share negative experiences. Instead, anticipate and prepare for them. Interviewers may ask difficult questions not so much for the substance of your answer but instead to see how you handle difficult questions. You may get questions about conflict with co-workers, job tasks that you didn't like doing, mistakes that you have made, or supervisors whom you didn't like or who didn't like you. Do not share the identity of the persons or organizations involved. Do share such instances if you are able, but when doing so, focus on how you handled the situation effectively rather than on the situation's negative impact. Do not leave the interviewers with the wrong impression that you were unable to proceed responsibly. Instead, share the strategies that you followed and tactics that you deployed that defused and corrected or improved the situation. Although it is less likely in an interview by lawyers than in interviews by others, you may even get inappropriate questions that implicate anti-discrimination laws, such as whether you are married or single, where you were born, and whether you have been arrested. Equal-employment-opportunity laws would permit you not to answer and would prohibit the employer from using an answer that you gave. Your issue, though, is whether to politely decline or to answer anyway, a judgment that may well depend on what your answer would reveal and how you think your answer would affect your employment prospects. If you decide not to answer, then consider politely asking the question's relevance to the job to alert your interviewer to its objectionable nature.

Asking Questions

Interviewers often ask if *you* have any questions for *them*. Be sensitive to what the interviewer truly expects. If the interviewer asks at the very end of the interview if you have any questions, then the question may just be a courtesy or pertain only to administrative things like next steps. In that instance, you need not and probably should not have any questions, unless you truly need some clarification. If instead the interviewer asks in mid-interview whether you have any questions about the job or firm, then the interviewer may well expect that you ask insightful questions showing your interest in the job and firm. You should then ask those questions, first about the job to confirm what you know about the job that fits your interest and qualifications, and then about the firm to show how well you know it from your research. Prefacing your job questions with *I understand that* and your employer questions with *I have seen that* will alert your interviewer that you have done your research. You may also add questions about clients, fields, and trends, prefaced with your insight that *it seems that* or *it looks like,* that again show your interest, research, and sophistication. Prepare these job, employer, and field or trend questions in advance. You do also have the opportunity in interview to ask questions that will help you decide whether to take an offered job. Those questions may include why the firm has an opening, what challenges the firm faces, who are its prime competitors, what are the job's typical activities, with whom you would be working, what training the employer will provide, how the employer will evaluate you, and what opportunities for promotion or professional development the position presents. Whether you ask these do-I-really-want-the-job questions may depend on how badly you need the job and whether you think that you have an offer coming.

Other Interview Conduct

The above sections have already given you good guidance on how to conduct yourself during an interview. Consider here some interview-behavior specifics, likely confirming things that you already know. As already mentioned above, common advice is to *be yourself,* which is fine if you are a thoughtful, polite, friendly, diplomatic, and engaging personality. If you aren't those things, then try to be. Don't be yourself if you are instead a bored, disinterested, disrespectful, and curmudgeonly gossip or grouch. If interviewing makes you nervous, then reduce nervousness by preparing, getting enough sleep the night before, allowing yourself extra time to dress and travel to the interview, focusing on the interviewer rather than yourself, and admitting to yourself and others that you are *excited,* not nervous. Of course, say nothing but the truth about yourself and your qualifications. Exaggeration, even on small points, doesn't help but instead hurts. Interviewers can often tell when a candidate exaggerates, having read the candidate's resume closely while perhaps also knowing something substantial of the candidate's background or special qualifications. Indeed, if the interviewer exaggerates your qualifications even on a small point, then correct the interviewer. While you may be diminishing what the interviewer believes to be your qualifications, you are simultaneously demonstrating your honesty and integrity even when against your interests. Do not criticize others, especially former employers but even also your prospective employer's competitors, even if the interviewer appears to invite you to do so. Keep things positive in all respects. If an interview question demands that you speak negatively about a person, organization, circumstance, or event, then do so reservedly and circumspectly, not emotionally or vengefully, grinding the proverbial axe. Certainly, do not denigrate other candidates, but also do not compare yourself overly favorably to the presumed class of candidates. You probably don't know who else has applied, and even if you do, then touting yourself over those candidates may come off as arrogance. Do not correct your interviewer on irrelevant points or opinions, or otherwise try to intimidate or demonstrate superior standing over your interviewer. You may be a lawyer, and your interviewer may not be, but a law degree and license are not permission to be rude and condescending. If your interview includes a meal, then treat the whole meal as an interview. Order something easy to eat, typically food that you would eat with utensils rather than your hands (such as ribs or a sloppy sandwich). As the interview wraps up, ask politely about next steps in the process, without presuming that your candidacy will advance to next steps. No matter how you feel the interview went, smile, shake hands, and thank the interviewer appreciatively at its conclusion.

Interview Follow Up

Ordinarily, you should expect that when your interview or interviews for a job are complete, that you would hear reasonably promptly from the employer as to whether you have advanced to any next steps. Ensure that the employer has your correct contact information and that you are indeed available and checking for that communication. One good way to do so, beyond just orally confirming that information as your interview manager shows you off the premises after the interview, is to leave your card. You should also write a prompt thank-you note for the interview no matter how you felt it went or how soon you expect to hear. Your thank-you note should be entirely gracious and appreciative, while also including your card or otherwise discretely including your contact information. Then, don't miss the employer's email, text, or call communicating the interview results and employer's decision, offer, or next steps, especially if you clarified with the employer that specific means of contact. Interview managers will routinely estimate for you how soon you should expect to hear. If your interview manager does not do so, and you have a special reason to need to know how soon you will hear back from the employer after interview, then you may ask your interview manager how soon you will hear, being sure not to sound desperate to know. Respect the employer's deliberative process. Unfortunately, follow-up communication from your prospective employer sometimes occurs later than you would expect or wish, and even later than the interview manager estimated. Sometimes a candidate will not hear from the employer following an interview, for a long enough period to cause the candidate to wonder whether the candidate would ever hear. Renewing polite communications with your interview manager, such as a brief note *just checking on status*, is appropriate as long as you are confident that you are not pressing for a decision that the employer is not ready to make. If you need a decision that the employer is not ready to make, then the employer's decision will be to reject you for the job.

Reference Checks

So, you get the employer's call after the last interview. Be ready for it. Rehearse how you will respond to what you might hear. A common and welcome next step following the interview or interviews, indeed the one that you most hope, is that the employer asks you to provide or confirm specific reference-check information. Such requests often mean that you have the job subject to positive references, although the employer may qualify that they are still considering multiple candidates while relying now on references to distinguish among closely qualified candidates. Again, be ready for it. Have a well-formatted, typewritten list of the name, title, firm, telephone, and email address of each professional whom you put forward as a reference. Choose and list from three to five references, no more and no fewer unless the employer asks for a specific number, in which case supply that specific number, no more and no fewer. Choose professionals whom the employer will most respect, routinely well-respected lawyers or judges, including law professors and deans, but only those who know enough about you to be a reliable reference, particularly those who have seen you do well what the job will require. Some of the best references can come from law professors for whom you were a teaching or research assistant, or who coached your competition team or supervised you in the law clinic, and lawyer supervisors at your internship. Do not list a reference without checking with the professional first. Also be sure that you have direct line or cell phone numbers available for each reference that you want the employer to reach promptly. Print the list on the same paper that you used for your resume. Do not submit the list with your resume unless the job application required you to do so. Let your references know to expect the employer's call.

Other Next Steps

Another common and welcome next step is that the employer asks you to authorize transcript, background, or records checks with your law school, undergraduate college or university, state or local bars or other professional associations, previous employers, credit bureaus, and police agencies, again often indicating that you have the job subject to confirmation of the qualifications, performance, character, and fitness that your application materials indicated. Again, be ready for it. Promptly execute at the employer's request the necessary authorizations for release of that information. Be especially prepared, though, for an actual job offer, which after all is your goal. How to respond to a job offer is the subject of **Step 8**. First, though, consider other very necessary interim and transition issues in **Step 8**.

STEP 8:

Manage Transition Issues

Your Transition Matters

The excitement and urgency of a job search can distract you from attending to important transition issues. The success of your job search depends in part on how well you manage those transition issues even as you conduct and complete your job search. While you search for a job, life goes on. You continue to need housing, food, transportation, and healthcare, which means that you continue to need household income. You also need to continue to maintain important familial and social responsibilities and relationships. Law students graduating from law school and transitioning into law careers also face unique transition requirements. If you intend to practice law, then you may register early or late for a state bar, apply for state-bar membership including completing onerous character-and-fitness certifications, and then of course register for the bar exam and prepare and pass the exam, all while completing graduation requirements and dealing responsibly with pending student-loan obligations. If your graduation means moving back to your home region or to a new destination, then you also have the many substantial responsibilities of that move beginning with relinquishing old and procuring new housing, moving personal property and persons, changes of address, and on and on. Don't ignore the transition issues. When left unattended, transition issues can complicate, limit, burden, and even defeat your job search. Recognize and respect the time, energy, and attention that you will need to attend to transition issues.

Record Transition Issues

Throughout your job search, from beginning through middle all the way to the end, use this **Step 8** to record, monitor, and attend to those transition issues so that your job search is easier and an ultimate success. Transition issues bedevil job searchers precisely because they are so fluid. You may have to coordinate multiple fixed-period obligations like apartment leases, cable-television contracts, vehicle registrations, health-clinic or health-insurance contracts, and daycare agreements or preschool tuition, with your changing job plans to relocate, move, downsize, take temporary quarters, or make other contingency plans as your job opportunities arise, shift, and finally settle into a career. You will have days when you feel like everything is in the air and nothing settled. You therefore need a place to turn where you can have a sense of control and order. Your **Step 8** electronic job-search journal is that place where you record every such transition issue, opportunity, thought, detail, and concern. For instance, events may spur you to take a half day to investigate and confirm contingency short-term housing in the new area to which you expect to move for your anticipated new job. Immediately write down in **Step 8** everything that you did and learned that half day. A week or two later, or a month or two later, when you need to execute swiftly and surely that short-term housing plan, you will have the information that you need in the place that you can find it. Whatever transition issue that you face, write it down in **Step 8** the moment that you think of it. Capture, record, and organize a body of information, plans, and actions to address it. Then, when your time is to act, you will act wisely and with planned effect. Consider some of the common transition issues.

Law Licensure

Surely the biggest transition issue for most law graduates transitioning to careers has to do with law licensure. The licensure challenge for lawyers is greater than for other licensed professionals because of the process's unfairly arduous nature, uncertainty, length, and locality. The first big licensure transition issue has to do with where you will work, requiring which state's license. Be especially strategic here. Do not register and seek licensure in a state on a whim that you'd always wanted to live there even though you've never been there, or on a tip that a certain employer may have your dream job. Depending on several variables only some of which you control, at least months and perhaps even years can elapse between the moment you decide to enter law practice in a certain state and the moment that the bar actually admits you in that state. Think of it: because of the cost, time, trouble, and bar-passage that licensure takes, most lawyers only ever license in one state. Choose carefully. Graduation may be your best time in life to make a major geographic move. Still, check it out thoroughly first. Once you have chosen your licensure state, though, then attack the licensure transition issue with the same energy and discernment that you approach your job search. In **Step 8**, record every step that your investigation shows that you must take, along with every action that you take to implement and execute that step. Stay on top of licensure. States offer the bar exam only twice each year. Do not find your job delayed by six months or lost entirely because you failed to manage licensure as a transition issue, timely and successfully. See the book *Preparing for the Bar Exam* and other similar resources for more details.

Finances

To continue and succeed in your job search, you must deal responsibly with your finances. Develop and record in **Step 8** a transition budget. Budgeting is neither rocket science nor hidden art. Simply think about what expenses you may incur each month as you pass from law school to career. The more uncertain you are about the answer, the more that you should commit to making estimates. Once you project monthly costs, then compare those costs to your household income and savings over the same period. If you are going to fall short in being able to pay expenses, then examine how you can reduce expenses and increase income. Job searching sounds like a bad time to be trying to earn supplemental income, but continuing a current part-time transitional job can give you that little bit of extra income that you may need, while not unduly distracting or burdening you. You may instead find that you can do some new contract online research, drafting, or document-review work that earns you some income on flexible at-home times while gaining you some valuable practice. If work is out of the question, then gifts or loans from family or others may be available. The point is to think it through and do your best rather than ignore finances. Your transition from law school to career may be the point of your lowest net worth, when you feel financial strain greater than ever. Yet that same moment is the point of your greatest earning potential, when you should feel most confident of the financial success that is ahead of you. Managing finances wisely during your transition, through your **Step 8** record, will help give you that confidence. Nearly every rich lawyer whom you know or have met started the same way. Start wisely.

Housing

Everyone has to live somewhere. Housing is a substantial essential, the most significant and hard-with-which-to-deal need. The two main transition issues that law graduates have with housing are (1) not enough and (2) too much. Because housing is so substantial, permanent, closely connected with personal welfare, and costly, housing tends to be a longer-term commitment. Housing is hard to get in and hard to get out, which again is why housing is a critical transition issue. Your earliest concern is that you be able to get out of the housing that you are

99

in at the time that you need to transition to another location to search for or accept a job. Don't purchase housing or sign a long-term lease when the housing's sale or lease termination would take longer than your earliest departure date. You don't want to pay for housing twice. If your current housing has only an annual lease renewal that would take you well beyond your departure date, then you may need to consider moving into temporary, transitional housing at your current location even before locating and committing to new housing at your job destination. Make **Step 8** plans with the strategies of minimizing cost and risk, while also mitigating disruption. Generate, record, and pursue options, such as subletting or storing personal property while rooming, that give you the greatest flexibility to pursue and take the best job. Don't get stuck taking a job that you don't want because you had inflexible housing. Also, don't commit too early to housing at your desired destination. Don't buy or lease long term just because jobs seem plentiful somewhere. Indeed, don't buy or lease long term too quickly after accepting a desirable job offer until you are sure that you like the job and the employer values you. Your housing mantra should be *light, inexpensive, and flexible*. You can put down deep roots later, well after a successful job search.

Health

Your mental and physical health should be one of your bigger transition concerns during your job search. We all find times when we may feel that we can or must sacrifice personal health habits for the good of the moment. Law school exams and bar-exam preparation may be two examples of times of anticipated personal sacrifice, when their stakes and challenges warrant a little less exercise, a little less sleep, and a little worse diet. The opposite may actually be true, that exams of any kind are a good time to give *more* rather than less attention to personal health. Whether or not that is so, don't make the mistake of sacrificing your personal health for time and attention to a job search. Yes, to undertake a successful job search, you may have to forgo training for your next triathlon. You may not be able to sleep in until noon every weekend or entertain friends for five-course home-cooked health-food meals. But during a job search, you can and should continue basic good exercise, rest, and diet habits. You have at least two good reasons to be especially healthy during a job search. One reason is that a job search takes mental and physical energy, vitality, and creativity. Fatigue, poor health, and depression make a job search hard or impossible. A second reason is that the interview process can readily expose your poor mental and physical health to prospective employers. You want and need to look, feel, and sound your best in interviews. Poor mental and physical health make it impossible to do so. Maintaining good health also includes having access to healthcare services. Do not cavalierly allow student or other transitional health-clinic or health-insurance benefits lapse on the expectation that your coming employer will soon have you covered. Also try not to forgo either routine or acute medical or dental care during a job search. Play it safe so that you are able to show up for interview and work both hale and hearty. Use **Step 8** of your job-search journal to record and monitor health, healthcare, and health-insurance issues, and investigate and implement transition actions to maintain your health.

Relationships

Among the easiest things to overlook during a job search, and most hazardous to overlook, are your family and social relationships. Your spouse is more important than your next job. So are your children, and so would be an elderly parent, disabled sibling, or other family member who depends on you and has no one else for care. On the other hand, your complaining aunt or conniving uncle does not hold hostage your career. While you should recognize and uphold your true family commitments, you should not sacrifice a career that could greatly benefit you and your family simply because a non-dependent family member attempts to exercise undue influence. The point is to prioritize thoughtfully and soundly. Any job decision that you make with your spouse's welfare first in mind is likely to be the right one. Never divorce or give grounds for divorce or separation just for a job. Involve your spouse or significant other in your decision where to move and for what kind of job. Listen closely, and make a joint decision about location and conditions such as compensation, benefits, and hours. In your transition, recognize the multiple familial, social, and other roles that you may hold including parent, child, spouse, sibling, student, teacher, worker, citizen, neighbor, friend, team member, coach, mentor, protégé, and adherent.

Fielding an Offer

Use **Step 8** to prepare yourself to field an offer, making notes of how you want to respond. You have worked hard to earn an offer. Don't spoil that hard work by letting an offer catch you flat footed and unprepared. Stumbling over an offer can cause an employer to hesitate, reconsider, and even withdraw the offer. Many employers prefer to telephone with an offer because of the personal touch that doing so conveys. Feel free, indeed be sure, to convey your pleasure and even excitement when you get that call. Be entirely appreciative and gracious, even if, indeed especially if, the call conveys terms that you did not expect, alters or contradicts terms that you did expect, or otherwise does not meet with your full approval. Avoid reacting to unexpected or undesired terms. Your purposes in fielding an offer should be simply to confirm the offer, confirm its material terms, and determine how soon you must and should respond, not yet to negotiate other terms. Before receiving an offer call, make a **Step 8** list of the terms that you need to know so that when you receive the call, you can refer to that list. The caller may tell you material terms including whether an associate position is on or off the partnership track, which practice group the position serves, compensation level, bonus eligibility, benefits, start date, and office location (assuming multiple office sites). If not, then you may politely and diplomatically ask, not in the nature of a demand or negotiation but again simply to confirm the terms. The caller should add that the firm will convey the complete terms in writing. If not, then you may politely and diplomatically ask whether you may expect an email or other writing summarizing the terms. The key, though, is to find out how quickly the employer expects you to respond. Employers can vary in their timetables. Some may need to rush a hire, while others prefer that you have *and take* deliberation time. Find out in the telephone call. Generally, you should not respond to an offer, either accepting or rejecting it, in the first call. To do so exhibits haste and disrespect for a deliberative process. If the caller appears to expect an immediate acceptance, then simply ask how long you may have so that you can speak to your spouse or other advisors. You may in that circumstance even suggest a brief response period such as 24 hours. If instead you get an email or other written offer as your first notice of an offer, then read it carefully for the response time. If you expect another, better offer from another, preferred employer, then consider asking for an extended response time such as a week. But when doing so, avoid giving as the reason that you are hoping for a better offer.

Decide—Wisely

The prior paragraphs intimate your biggest transition issue: deciding whether to take a job offer and, if you have more than one offer, which offer to take. You may not have to jump at the first offer. You may have time to deliberate before you decide. Indeed, especially when you don't have deliberation time, you should have thought in advance about how you will decide whether to take a job offer. So as you begin and pursue your job search, think from time to time about how you should decide whether to take a certain offer. You may realize, for instance, that you should speak first to a former faculty advisor, lawyer mentor, or wise relative to see what they think about a certain offer. You may decide to pray, meditate, or imagine yourself in the job, and then see how you feel. You may decide to share news of the offer with an old law school or college friend to see how the friend reacts. You may remember to look carefully at your financial plan to see how the offer's financial terms affect your financial future. In your decision-making process, decide how much you should value strategies like optimism versus pessimism, flexibility versus the discipline to stick to criteria, persistence versus the willingness to change, curiosity versus affinity, and risk taking versus minimizing risk. Stick to your plan, but be ready to accept fortuitous happenstance. Visualize yourself in the new job going through what you believe would be a typical workday, and then share your impression with the person to whom you are closest. As you think of these things throughout your job search, record them here in **Step 8** of your electronic job-search journal. Then, when your time to decide arrives, you will have abundant thoughtful guidance for how to decide. Think in advance about how to go about deciding, and you will make a better decision when the time comes. With whom among family, friends, and mentors should you speak about an offer? Be prepared. Do not let a job offer take you by surprise. Review your commitments listed in **Step 1**. Refer to this section whenever you feel that you may soon get an offer and when you do get an offer.

An Offer Is Not an Acceptance

You will get a job offer or multiple job offers. Your job search will produce results, positive results. When you get what is or what looks like an offer, expect to be joyous, excited, proud, and elated. Expect to celebrate and rejoice. Do not, however, mistake a job offer as your acceptance. Just because an employer finds you better qualified and a more desirable candidate than other candidates, and extends an offer for a certain position, presumably the position for which you applied, does not mean that the offer binds you to accept it. You may be tempted to communicate an immediate acceptance, the moment that you get the call, text, or email conveying the offer, as if doing so is your only possible option or appropriate response. Stop. No matter what the caller told you in conveying an oral offer, read and carefully consider the terms, tone, and conditions of the written offer that you will actually accept or reject. The offer may clearly communicate that the employer expects you to take at least some time, whether a day or two or longer, to decide whether to accept the offer. The communication may also leave open additional material terms yet to negotiate, making your rushed acceptance an inappropriate stumble. Remember to think about your decision-making process, referring to the notes that you made about it here in **Step 8** of your job-search journal. Make a thoughtful, considered, logical, reasoned, and planned decision, not an agonizing, impulsive, or fatalistic decision. Gut feelings are worth considering as long as you can justify your gut. Do not procrastinate over the decision, and do not let an offer paralyze you. Do not let others tell you what to do, but do listen to their counsel. You have a lawyer's training. Use it. Gather information about the offer and offeror, review your decision criteria, weigh the offer and alternatives, choose soundly with appropriate counsel, and then take prompt action.

Beware the Counteroffer

While communicating in ways that clarify the offer may be perfectly appropriate, sensible, and even expected, be cautious about replying with anything that looks not like a question or clarification but more like a counteroffer. You know the law: a counteroffer constitutes rejection. Some employers may accept or even expect a counteroffer, entertaining negotiation over compensation, benefits, relocation expenses, or other terms and conditions. Other employers do not accept or appreciate counteroffers, and do not countenance negotiations. Those employers may firmly and politely reject your attempt to negotiate, while holding the offer open. Or those employers may construe your attempt to negotiate as a *faux pas* warranting their withdrawal of the offer. It happens. Many employers take great pride in their enterprise, treating employees as family. Some of those employers may feel that you shouldn't negotiate with family and may take a counteroffer as an indication that you are not sufficiently trusting of their future care. The bottom line is that if you feel that you must negotiate for better terms, then be ready to find another job. You are completely free to do so, and you may be doing the right thing. Just don't regret your attempt if it loses you a position that you later feel you should have accepted on the offered terms.

Evaluating Compensation

As already indicated just above, you should use your **Step 1** commitments to evaluate the offer. What, though, about the offer's financial terms, particularly compensation? Information is power. You should have available for your consideration reliable state bar or other information on compensation for the position's geographic locale, firm size, and practice field. Many state bars periodically collect and publish that information, making it available online at least to members and possibly also to the public. The Bureau of Labor Statistics also publishes wage information, while your law school's career office will also have helpful wage data. Do your research. Compare your offer to average and median compensation in your field. Remember, though, to use compensation ranges and to adjust averages and medians down to your starting status and limited experience. Lawyer income tends to go up and often go up dramatically across the course of a career, particularly in the first five, ten, or fifteen years, when annual income may double, triple, or more. Do not reject out of hand an offer the compensation for which is substantially below the median, if circumstances look like you can earn your way to and above the median over reasonable time. Also, listen carefully for information on annual year-end bonuses. Many firms compensate at lower salaries but then increase the compensation substantially, by ten or twenty percent or more, even in some cases doubling a salary or more with year-end bonuses, depending on the firm's profit in that year. Listen carefully, too, for information on whether bonuses are merit based or spread equally across employee levels, particularly if you have reason to believe that you will perform at a significantly higher or lower productivity as other employees at your level. Employers may share bonus criteria reluctantly when making an offer, but use what information you glean to estimate your total annual compensation, bonuses included. Benefits also make a great difference in the value of a compensation package, on average increasing that value by around twenty-five percent. An offer should include a reliable description of benefits. Price the value of provided benefits and also omitted-but-necessary benefits so that you have a full understanding of the offer's value. Make informed decisions using available and reliable data.

Negotiating Terms

If the employer is willing and you need or want to do so, countenancing the risks, then don't hesitate to negotiate over employment terms before accepting an offer. Some employers feel that a candidate demonstrates valuable confidence and job skill when negotiating over the candidate's own employment terms. Indeed, if the offer indicates only a salary range rather than a specific figure, then the employer has just invited your negotiation. Yet do not make a game or test of wills and negotiating skill out of salary negotiation. A negotiation over compensation is not at arm's length. You may very soon be working very closely with the persons on the other side of the negotiation, needing their utter trust. Never exaggerate or mislead, such as to suggest that you have another offer when you don't or make more money already than you actually do. If you discern that your qualifications place you only at the bottom of an offer's salary range, then invite the employer to set the specific figure and accept the specific figure that the employer establishes. Who knows but that the employer may set a higher-than-low-end figure? You may respond to an offered range with a range of your own that is higher than but also overlaps the employer's range, in which case the employer may suggest the lowest figure in your range. You'd then need to accept that figure because you effectively set it. Or you may instead ask what you would need to demonstrate in order for the employer to compensate you at a higher level within the range. The employer may name qualifications that you already have, earning you the higher starting salary. If at any point the employer gives you a non-negotiable figure that you are reluctant to accept but feel that you must do so, then consider asking for a sooner-than-annual compensation review, say in three or six months. And if the money isn't quite right but the employer won't budge, then consider negotiating for compensatory terms like a performance bonus, flexible schedule, telecommuting (work-from-home) day, or specific professional development opportunities.

Rejecting an Offer

As hard as you may have worked to find a job, you still should not feel as if you must accept any offer. Some offers you should not accept, for instance to associate with a lawyer whose discipline record and reputation indicate incompetence or dishonesty. You should also not accept an offer of a job for which you are not qualified unless the employer is clear and genuine in its commitment to train you. You should also not accept an offer of a job that does not provide you with a sustainable living, although some such jobs may provide a stepping stone to a job that will sustain you. Refer to your **Step 1** commitments to ensure that you can accept a job offer without destroying or unduly burdening those commitments. If you do decide to reject an offer, then do so in an entirely respectful correspondence that first thanks the employer for the offer, then thanks any specific individuals who helped you through the candidate process, and concludes repeating the appreciation. Do not respond negatively, even if something or someone in the offer or process treated you unfairly. After all, the employer made an offer. If you feel that you need to report the unfairness or should do so, then communicate those offenses to your law school's career office so that you can have the career official's counsel and so that the career official can either communicate with the employer without disclosing your identity, take the offense into account in advising and referring future candidates, or help you navigate diplomatic communications with the rejected employer. Although you have rejected the employer's offer, the employer may improve the offer. Don't burn bridges unnecessarily.

Accepting an Offer

If you do decide to accept an offered position, then do so both orally or by email as the offer and its timing may have implied or expressly invited but also with a formal acceptance letter. Make sure, of course, to accept within any imposed timeline. Do not, in other words, accept a day or week later than the offer required. Direct your acceptance to the person who made the offer or other person to whom that person directed you to respond. In your oral, email, and letter acceptances, begin with generous appreciation for the offer along with an entirely positive expression of your future employment. You may then very briefly summarize any key employment terms, particularly any material terms that the employer conveyed only orally, negotiated with you but did not confirm in the written offer, or otherwise left out of or left ambiguous in the written offer. Your start date is a good example of a material term to confirm, particularly if in oral communications the employer agreed to delay or accelerate that date. Close the letter with a third and final paragraph that repeats your appreciation for the offer and excitement over starting with the employer. As with any other correspondence in your job search, proofread, proofread, proofread, while following all other protocols and conventions for business correspondence. In replying orally and in writing, you may feel as if you can now relax, let your proverbial guard down, and communicate informally as if you are a trusted part of your new team. You are a trusted part of your new team, but your acceptance letter is not the time or place to assume informal communication styles. You are still performing a professional function when accepting a job offer. Act professionally in your communications with your about-to-be employer. Have fun alone or with friends and family at home.

Start Off Right

Another objective, indeed a final objective that you want to achieve in your job search transition is to start off the new job right. Surprising as it may seem, you should be thinking and planning now, not at the last minute, in order to start your new job right. Whenever you feel down about your job search, picture yourself starting the new job. Think, then, of how you want to feel. List now, here in **Step 8,** how you want to start the new job. Include not just what *you* want but what *your employer* would want, meaning the character, habits, and attitude that employers prefer in new employees. First impressions are important. Getting off on the right foot is important. Remember that you never get a second chance to make a first impression. What will make your first day on the job, your first week on the job, your first month and year most successful and satisfying? Your answer may depend on your health, relationships, finances, spirit, and state of mind. Your job search need not be like a marathon in which you limp to the end completely spent of all vital resources. Your job search should be a satisfying, exciting, and fulfilling process that prepares you for your new job. You should know and meet both your own expectations and your new employer's expectations. Review, reflect on, and add to this section whenever you get excited about finding your new job or feel that you need to regain that excitement.

Navigate the New Job

So, you earned the new job that you wanted, and you came prepared to start off right. How, though, do you actually navigate the first day, week, month, or season at the new job? Job searchers both win *and lose* new jobs, sometimes all in just a week or month. New employees also sometimes navigate the new job so poorly that they take much longer than necessary to fit in and adjust. Consider this advice. First, while your energy level will initially be high and you will naturally want to show how productive and effective you can be, you are probably better to start a little slow than to start too fast, meaning to take on too much. New employees should follow the rule to first do no harm. When you don't yet know the firm's standards, policies, and protocols, you are better to navigate with care and caution so as not to create a problem where no problem existed. Your job as a lawyer is to solve problems rather than create them. Don't make a mess. Second, keep your eyes open and your mouth shut. Watch and learn, don't preach and burn. Third, show extra grace to others rather than expecting others to extend grace to you. Your experienced co-workers will likely be extra patient with and supportive of you. If they aren't, then ignore their impatience or insult rather than react to it. New employees don't usually pull their own weight. Respect that others are pulling your weight for you. Give them room even to grouse and complain about your unfamiliarity with the job's requirements. Don't take offense over it. Instead, notice their skill, thank them for their correction, and show that you are now ready to fulfill the job's full requirements. Fourth, don't make fast friends too quickly. *No romances.* Especially, don't join cliques or factions, especially ones that work against the firm's mission or boss. Fifth, welcome mentors both on and off the job. Seek them out, and learn from them. You may indeed be fully competent already, even more so than other members of the firm. Then again, you may not be, and you are not a good judge of your own competence. Rely on mentors to guide, save, and rescue you. Learn the firm's culture and politics. Conform to positive culture, while avoiding politics.

Continue Your Development

One of the best ways to ensure that you navigate, survive, and prosper in a new job is to continue your professional development. Lawyers tend to grow in their knowledge and skills exponentially in the first months and years of law practice, particularly when they have a strongly supportive professional network and frequent professional-development opportunities. Find out what professional-development activities your new employer prefers and supports. If the firm sends its lawyers to continuing-legal-education seminars, then apply to attend, even if still new on the job. Continuing legal education is not law school. Continuing-education seminars focus on narrow practice areas, current issues, and practical knowledge, tools, and solutions. One good day-long conference or seminar can and should teach you more about what you need to know to practice in a certain area than three years of law school taught you about that area. Join state bar sections relating to your new field to network with experienced practitioners and read section newsletters and updates. Get training within the firm in the software, technology, and systems that the firm's experienced employees use. Expand your systems and technology skills quickly so that you can use the productivity tools and follow the productive routines that more-experienced employees do. Associate with the more-engaged and more-productive partners and senior associates. When you have the opportunity to prioritize assigned work, then prioritize the work of those senior and skilled lawyers from whom you can learn the most and with whom you most want to work. And don't forget your law school professors, staff, and career office. They can both help you navigate troubled waters and speed your professional development in your chosen field.

Keep Your Balance

Keeping a semblance of work-life balance can be one of the harder things for a new lawyer to do. The problem is only in part the demands of the new employer. Many firms have learned that grinding up and spitting out large numbers of new associates is poor labor management, imposing high personal costs while lowering morale and producing high recruitment and training costs. Many other firms have always encouraged associates to maintain responsible work-life balance. Fewer firms require the long hours that tip that balance and can destroy mental or physical health and family and social relationships. The more-significant problem than firm-imposed time demands can be law practice's allure. Law practice is a window into reality, the kind of real issues, challenges, and opportunities that non-lawyers seldom see firsthand and can only barely imagine. Be excited about your new work and its significance, but don't let your excitement cause you to commit more time and energy to your job than you can sustain over time in healthy mind, body, and relationships. Slow down, at least evenings and weekends, to enjoy the rich perspective on practice. When in the office for longer days, get up and move around. When out of the office, make a priority of exercise, healthy food, and fun in important relationships. Have something, whether service project, faith community, arts or literature interest, or other hobby, activity, or recreation, that fully engages you outside of work, to give your mind and spirit a break from work's excitement. Observe how other lawyers in the firm maintain work-life balance, and emulate the best practices, especially how they manage time and tasks to keep work hours productive and reasonable. Every firm has its unhappy grinder, while every firm also has expert professionals who balance life and work. A few even have joyful and uplifting renaissance figures. Recognize that you largely control which character you will be. Set work goals, but also set personal goals. Set short-term goals, but also set long-term goals. Then find an accountability partner outside of the law firm to help you assess your balance and progress. Make sure that you have and nurture significant relationships, family and friends, outside of work relationships. Know who is important to you, and then treat them that way. And don't talk about work with family and friends.

Part II

Inspirational Proof

So you have the plan and program. Now you just need the proof and inspiration. As with anything, in a job search you must first believe that you can succeed before you will put forward the energy and practice the discipline to do so. Belief comes from proof. Proof, in the case of job search, comes from evidence that others have followed the same or similar plan with good results. The accounts collected here represent the actual stories of recent law school graduates. The accounts disguise to some degree each of the true stories in order to protect the successful job searcher's anonymity, even though many of those successes whom the accounts describe would gladly share their identity. They are pleased with and proud of their job search results, and want their results to encourage you. To a person, they would all say that because they succeeded, you can succeed, too. Of course, each successful job searcher offered their eventual employer something unique. Each also took a unique approach to their job search in certain respects. Yet each also more or less followed the steps of the plan that you have just reviewed. See how the following accounts can inspire and guide you in executing your own job-search plan. Refer to them freely and frequently. These accounts have just as much to teach you as the plan itself.

The Routine

In retrospect, after she had found, won, and for a time enjoyed her new job, her job search seemed to her to have been entirely ordinary in its every step, other than the last surprising one. She had not in her job search done anything special, only done the usual and routine. She had good qualifications, even if not spectacular. Nothing in the process had particularly surprised her, and nothing had felt later like it had been extraordinarily fortuitous, instead just predictable. While some of her classmates seemed to be going through great drama in their job searches, including peaks and valleys of stress and emotion, excitement and grief, her job search had instead been more like a cruise than a roller coaster. Things felt afterward as if they had simply fallen in place. She had a basically attractive resume, sound cover letter, good internship experience with a positive recommendation letter, decent writing sample, and solid grades, class standing, and service work. She had learned that a small but longstanding local municipal-law firm was hiring a new associate. She had applied without fanfare and received a prompt interview, warm welcome, and job offer at the interview's conclusion, which she had accepted as a matter of course, appreciatively but without giddiness or great elation. The only thing that hadn't been routine was her response to the work itself. She had enjoyed the work but still felt called to other things. So after a few months at the new job, she had spoken with the managing partner who had in their short time together been as much a mentor or even father figure to her as her employer. They agreed that she would work flexibly, part time, while she took on three other part-time jobs, each drawing on her different talents, each fulfilling its own call.

The Clerkship

He realized later that he must have had the least stressful of all possible job searches. Having mastered his first and second-term law school courses with unusual confidence and alacrity, he had applied to a local small but prominent litigation firm hoping to get a little experience as a law clerk while continuing his studies and before looking for his long-term job. As soon as he started at the firm, though, he realized that he may already have found that job. The firm's partners made no preliminary promises. He expected to the contrary that he had a long learning curve and much to prove before this prominent small firm would even consider him for permanent full-time employment. Yet the skill that he had shown in first-year courses transferred pretty readily to his law-clerk work. His equanimity when faced with multiple tasks and deadlines, his solid work habits, and his growing skill, combined with a stable and mature character, impressed the partners who gave him increasing responsibility. He continued to work for the firm part-time while in school and fulltime when not, including attending long trials for which he would take on extra work. He liked the work and partners, and the work and partners liked him. While he kept his resume fresh, explored various job listings, and didn't ignore that he might soon need to start a serious job search, everything that he was picking up from the partners indicated that he might well have a permanent fulltime job after graduation. Then the day came when the partners asked to meet with him about his future with the firm. What they proposed in the transition terms into that fulltime job nearly took him aback, the partners had been so thoughtful and sensitive. He accepted their generous offer promptly after consultation with his quite-happy wife. He still had to earn his way. He was only now a new associate. But he felt as if he had been with the firm forever, as indeed he had been for years. In retrospect, he couldn't think of a moment that had felt like a stressful job search.

The Star

From the start, she had every reason to believe that her job search would be fruitful, even if its course had seemed surprisingly eventful and uncertain. She supposed in retrospect that every job search must have its briefly harrowing moments, even if only in the exaggeratedly dramatic sense of first-world problems. Nothing had ever actually threatened her or her career. She had only had moments in her job search when she didn't exactly seem to have a career yet, only the continuing hope of a career. The uncertainty of her job search had been surprising because, again, she had every reason to believe that she was a strong, maybe even an *exceptional*, candidate. She had come to law school with outstanding academic credentials from a strong undergraduate program that was a feeder to professional schools. She was from a family of professionals and had from as early as she remembered anticipated her own professional career. She had found every success in law school that she had expected, and then some. The extra law school success that she had earned had been mostly through her teaching-assistant and research-assistant relationships with supportive faculty members. That work had led her to conference attendance, conference presentation, and even publication, unusual credits for a law student. She had interned at two major law firms and even had multiple interviews at large firms interested in her hot specialty-field focus. Still, until right around graduation, she had not yet landed an actual job. Then, finally, the welcome and well-earned offer came from a high-reputation insurance-defense firm with outstanding management and mentorship, and multiple offices in desirable locations. Her new job would draw heavily on her specialty focus. The firm would employ her part-time while she studied for the bar exam and full-time while she waited for the positive results. She was, indeed, a star, shining brightly right where she should have been.

The Circuitous

He hadn't foreseen that his job search would take so many major twists and turns. On entering law school, he had mistakenly assumed that law students just graduated and got jobs. He hadn't realized that law graduates had so many options, as did their employers. He didn't realize until later that getting a job with a law firm could be a bit more like a courtship and marriage than an arm's length transaction, indeed even in his case several courtships, one or two engagements, and then finally a lasting marriage. He hadn't thought in advance that he would need to think carefully about where he would license, who might employ him there, and how he would get to know that employer well enough to gain their confidence to hire him. His job search had worked out well enough in the long run, just that it had been a longer run with more wide curves and a few sharp ones that he hadn't anticipated. He had, in retrospect, chosen to license in the wrong state, a place that he and his wife had in the end decided not to remain, after he had worked there for only a few months. Having to license again in his home state had of course meant a major delay in resuming law practice, while he took and passed a second bar exam. When he did start again, the practitioner who hired him turned out to be more interested in business than law practice, which after a few more months meant that he was looking for the right job once again. One great connection with a fine small firm made him think he had an inside track, but the job never materialized. Then, after more than two years of these twists, turns, and seeming dead ends, all of which he had managed to fill with temporary and transitional employment, his law school's career office let him know that another position had just opened up with an outstanding lawyer whose lone associate had moved on to a larger firm. Within days, the successful courtship was over, and he was happily ensconced in a general practice for which all of his twists and turns had somehow perfectly prepared him. Only then did he realize that he wouldn't have become the lawyer that he was without that circuitous route to his career employment.

The Grinder

If he hadn't been such a realist, such a hard-nosed, pragmatic, school-of-hard-knocks character, then he would have had to pinch himself with how well his job search had worked out, to be sure that the results were real. He had been a hardworking just-talented-enough scholarship athlete in college but only until he blew out his knee and could no longer compete. He then worked his way through college, sleeping on friend's couches and working nights to avoid going deeply into debt. On college graduation, he took a traveling job opening small office franchises. Fortune then smiled on him so that he married the love of his life, whose ambition for him led him to law school. He did law school the same way that he did college, frugally and with hard work. So he knew exactly what to do for his job search: go find a solo practitioner who could show him law practice's ropes because he knew he'd soon be out on his own and certainly didn't expect anyone to hand him anything. He gussied up a resume and did the interviews, winning a solid internship with a premier solo practitioner in his hometown. As the internship proceeded, he continued to plan on starting his own law practice as soon as the internship ended, he graduated, and he passed the bar. Yet on his internship's last day, the senior solo practitioner offered him a salary nearly double what he might have expected, if he had expected anything, in order to stay on with the firm. Better yet, the solo practitioner would pay for his bar-review course and employ him as a law clerk until he got his bar results and joined the firm as its first new associate. He had more than earned the offer, the solo practitioner explained. And indeed, the next three years of law practice working for and with the premier solo practitioner were so much more rewarding and profitable than he could have expected if he had started out alone. He was so good at the work that he eventually did start his own firm even while maintaining very close professional relationship with the lawyer who had given him his start. Simply persevering in earnest without complaint, or *grinding* as he thought of it from his sports background, had worked.

The Niche

She had been concerned from the start of law school that she would need just the right law job in order for the whole law school pursuit to have worked. Her challenges included that she was a homemaker, indeed, the primary caretaker for the grade-school children whom she and her husband, a professional, were raising. She would be reentering the workforce after graduation, but even then, she would still have children for whom and home for which to care, not to mention also wanting to respect and support the career of her very successful husband. Because of her special job needs, she felt in retrospect that she had begun her job search on her first day of law school, when she had met women lawyer mentors at an orientation program. She began from that day forward to learn about practice areas, law firm and compensation arrangements, and other professional-career particulars that were more conducive to a balanced, mature, and responsible family life. If she was going to navigate effectively her time in the sandwich generation, caring not only for children but also elderly parents, spouse, and self, then she was going to have to recognize the priority of her various commitments and then match those priorities to the few law careers that might fit and serve them. On that first day of law school, though, she had already learned not only that successful career and life navigation were possible together but also that she now had clues as to how. Her mentors gradually guided her toward a transactional practice where she could limit her hours and control her schedule, rather than litigation practice, and then toward estate planning where the timetables and turnarounds are longer, rather than business planning. Her law school's career office, her own research, and her networking helped her connect with practitioners in that field whose practices were local to her geographic area. She then began to meet those practitioners, especially those who had the reputation of supporting and respecting new lawyers. At the same time, she took elective courses that would highly qualify her for that practice, while also choosing writing subjects and assignments that would produce tangible evidence of her skill for interested employers. Her break came when one of those local practitioners contacted her a term before graduation to see if she would be willing to take on part-time employment as a law clerk.

121

Her part-time work quickly convinced the practitioner that she was the perfect candidate for full-time employment following the bar exam. Years of satisfying and effective law practice later, she could easily attest that she had indeed found the perfect niche to both serve her community as a lawyer while also continuing her rich and responsible family and social life.

The Meticulous

She had been a very strong student academically, even if not in leadership, student or service activities, teamwork, faculty collaborations, or other campus life. She had simply stuck to herself, being respectful of others and their broader interests while focused like a laser on every little detail of her doctrinal studies. Her almost compulsive interest in the accuracy, clarity, and perfect form of everything that she heard, saw, produced, or touched took full flower in her writing courses. She quickly mastered the scrupulous skills for legal writing including both drafting and scholarly writing, for which she also had a keen mind. Students respected her even if they didn't particularly know her, as she homed in on and conquered with exquisite alacrity each individual task that the curriculum set before her. No one was surprised at her *summa cum laude* graduation. Nor were any surprised that while still in the middle of her third year of law school she had already located, clerked for, and duly impressed a mid-sized, nearly all-male firm of very fine and also very senior lawyers. She graciously accepted the firm's offer not only to employ her while she studied for the bar exam and waited for results but also to pay for her commercial bar-preparation course. In her first two years at the firm, her meticulous nature, keen mind for law doctrine, and honed technical skills, and the fast burn of her slightly compulsive nature, made her the firm's perfect, indeed star, associate. Word spread of her technical skill and productive capacity. While she loved her mid-sized firm and appreciated its confidence in her while she had still been a student, she could not resist the generous offer that the area's largest firm made to her for a lateral move. Her new employer gave her substantial responsibility working on even more highly technical matters for one of its longest-served and largest corporate clients. She thrived doing high-value work for which few other lawyers had the capacity.

The Reluctant

She had done alright in law school, she supposed, although she had very little sense of confidence or accomplishment. Among the many gunners, academic stars, overachievers, service saints, and student leaders who were her law school friends and peers, she felt *undistinguished*, ordinary, and overlooked. Her law school's programs, as many and laudable as they were, just hadn't really seemed to fit her ordinariness, her few mundane and quiet interests, comforts, and concerns. Then the realization had hit her: she was going to graduate and needed a job. Yet given her ordinariness, in her pre-graduation job search she felt as if she was just going through the ordinary motions. Having nothing to distinguish herself, she couldn't find any affinity or hook with which to connect her to any law firm opportunity. Her resume had no pop to it, nothing to make anyone take notice, and so as many resumes as she sent with her carefully crafted cover letter, she received no calls for interviews. She had no knack for networking, wasn't in any sense a self-promoter, and wasn't even comfortable making small talk. She couldn't even come up with an elevator talk about herself, try as she might to fashion and rehearse one. She did sign up for a couple of on-campus interviews, but her impression afterward was that the polite interviewers had looked past her almost as if she hadn't been in the room. So she did the only thing that she could do, which was to prepare for, take, and pass the bar exam, while she continued her fruitless job search. Her husband, a highly respected and fully extroverted supervisor in a very large workplace, was glad at her licensure. He could finally begin to refer to her his many friends and co-workers who had ordinary legal needs and who were looking for an ordinary, undistinguished, and trustworthy lawyer. After getting malpractice insurance and while still working from home, she took one matter, then another, then another, getting occasional guidance on these and other new matters from other recent alumni and her former law professors. Within a couple of months, she was leasing a small office. A couple more months later, she was starting to turn down and refer matters that didn't feel quite right, sensing that she could already be more selective. Within a couple more months, she could see that she had already developed a solid practice mix in three or four related areas. Her clients, she found, didn't want or need a standout lawyer. They needed an ordinary lawyer to do ordinary work that served their ordinary lives. As it turned out, her job search had proven perfectly successful. It had turned her right back to discovering who she was and where she was in an ordinary but very satisfying world.

The Planner

He had always been a planner. Indeed, before the advent of laptops, tablets, and smartphones, when he had started his career in business, he had carried and heavily used a planner, even when he started law school. He had gone to law school because his mentor in business had a law degree and thought that a law degree would be good for his business career, too. He hadn't planned to change jobs after law school. He was just going to use the law degree to advance his position in the thriving business for which he worked under that great mentor. Yet late in his third law school year, the economy hit a rough patch, and the business, to his shock, closed. He felt that he had no option other than to go into law practice, with which he was fine, given that his interest in and skill for law had vastly grown. Although he hadn't planned to lose his job and wasn't happy about it, he was nonetheless a little relieved and excited that he had a new future before him in law. The problem, though, was that he hadn't done anything to plan for it, when his nature was to plan. So he hastily put together a resume and began working with the law school's career office to look for a law job, even as he prepared for and took the bar exam. Yet even as he began his job search, late and without any preliminary networking or other adequate preparation, something told him that he should begin first in solo practice. He had, after all, run a business as second in command under his business mentor. He felt that he should test his business acumen in this new law field and put his business-management skills to good use. So although he did an abbreviated job search just to see what might be out there, he instead put his full planning efforts into starting a solo practice. He wanted a sure thing, not the chance for a job, and he just felt that he was well positioned for solo success. And succeed he did, managing to build a high-end estate-planning practice within just a couple of years that kept him and a legal assistant gainfully employed. He even began taking interns from the law school so that he could employ his first associate. Yet in all the satisfaction of building his own professional practice, he missed the sense of organizational loyalty that he had when in business. He realized that he wanted to be part of something bigger. He also wanted to more easily take a vacation and otherwise share the responsibilities of managing a firm. So with a minimum of networking, he joined a thriving mid-sized firm in a lateral move that brought the firm his own substantial book of high-end estate-planning business. He hadn't really planned his job search, but his planning skills had helped him build a practice that made his job search easy.

The Perseverant

His path into, through, and out of law school, and into his dream law job, hadn't been easy, that much he knew. He was just glad in hindsight that he hadn't known in advance those many twists and turns, or he might not have persisted or even begun. He had made a considered and, he thought at the time, *wise* choice to go to law school. Indeed, his wisdom had proven itself correct in the long run, once he had won his very-desirable job with which he was absolutely delighted. At nearly every point along the way, though, his choice had looked more hazardous than wise, from precisely that job perspective. No sooner had he begun than he began to doubt that his law school could actually get him the job that he had expected. The school's faculty and staff were optimistic and encouraging, particularly given his early academic proficiency, not outstanding but good enough for confidence. The school had thousands of employed alumni, many of them prominent judges and practitioners, and the educational program was rigorous and quality throughout. But the economy was still recovering, and he found plenty of fuel for doubt about job prospects, among senior (some would say *cranky*) lawyers in the field not to mention his more-anxious classmates. Late in his first year, he decided to transfer to another ostensibly more-prominent law school. He knew nearly the moment that he got there that he had made a bad choice. By his third year, he was back at his original law school, fortunately in time to serve an internship at a local premier mid-sized law firm. He knew when the law firm accepted him for the internship that it had no plan on offering him a job. The hiring partner told him so in what at the time had felt like a crushing blow. Yet he gambled that the firm's very strong reputation and very skilled lawyers would help him get a job at another firm, especially if he learned everything that he could from the internship. His internship work earned him rave reviews but, as he expected, no job offer. He made a point, though, of being as gracious as humanly possible in appreciation for the internship. He knew that he had made not only believers out of the firm's key partners but also some friends among staff and associates whose jobs he had deliberately and skillfully made easier. He had nothing left to do than prepare for the bar exam while putting out resumes, neither a particularly attractive task. If nothing else, though, he had learned to persevere, right through the bar exam, which he felt that he had aced. Yet no sooner was the exam over than he got the firm's call with an offer, although only for contract work, making for another good news/bad news twist to his job search. He took the offer with all the grace that he could once again muster and applied himself to the job as diligently as he would have if they had installed him in a corner office in partnership. Lo and behold, barely a couple of months passed before the firm converted him to an associate position. A year later, he still had to pinch himself to believe that his persevering job search had ended so exquisitely well.

The Fortunate

He had never really worried about getting a job out of law school. Maybe the reason had been because he had worked his way through law school. In fact, he had worked *nights* all the way through law school. So he could in retrospect have felt that he had earned the job, indeed the *jobs* (plural) that he got after law school. But he didn't feel that way, certainly didn't feel entitled to a law job. Rather, he just felt fortunate, blessed, well-off, and even a little privileged. Working nights had relieved him of any illusions that the world owed him anything, even a job after graduation. His first law job after graduation had felt like an absolute stroke of fortune. Because he had kept his night job right up until graduation, he had decided to delay taking the bar exam until its next administration by which time he could prepare properly. Fortune's stroke gave him a family court mediator's job—a *day* job!—at the courthouse in the meantime, while he studied. Of course, no job comes about entirely by chance. His supervisor at the courthouse was also a relatively recent graduate of his law school, one who now taught the law school's students in bar-exam skills. He had evidently impressed her in and around the class. His full-time mediator job then became the perfect transition from studying for the bar to waiting for results and then stepping into his next law job, indeed his dream job, as a public defender. And again, while his new public-defender job felt at the time like another stroke of great fortune, in fact while in law school he had interned for the public-defender's office where he had evidently impressed the chief defender. The fortune was only in the perfect timing of the opening of an assistant defender's job just as he had gotten his bar results. He had done the right things in planning and preparing for his job search, and then in executing it. His law school competition successes, skills coursework, internship, and networking, and even his bar studies, had all proven to be just the right steps in just the right order with just the right timing. He had in some manner planned everything that way, although his job search had in the end come together feeling as if it was simply great good fortune.

The Classmate

Although the dean and his professors had been telling him from the start of law school on, he hadn't fully realized how significant his classmates could be in influencing his career path. He had been a strong student academically, and also mature, productive, disciplined, and experienced enough in the world's ways, that he hadn't worried much about winning a job. He sensed from the start of law school that he was going to land with a law firm that he was over the long term likely to make a lot of money while providing a lot of good service to its profitable corporate clients. Not many of his classmates seemed to have that confidence or, indeed, that interest. He was comfortable enough with the possibility of joining a profitable corporate-services law firm, though, that he continued to pursue that possibility throughout law school. Early on, he researched the local area's law firms, picking out a couple that he thought would make the best landing place. He then worked with his professors not only to identify lawyers in those firms with whom he could meet but to help him use the law school's courses and programs to build the kind of resume that would open the door to a job at one of those firms. His networking with the firms paid off first in a clerkship and then, well before graduation, in a very attractive job offer. The offer was so attractive that he jumped at it without thinking about his life goals, lifestyle, commitments, interests, or alternatives. He wasn't a particularly reflective person. He instead tended in every situation to respond to others' needs.

And law school had somehow shaped him into serving the needs of corporate clients through profitable law firms. These things he only realized later, two-plus years into his law firm job, when he got a call from a law school classmate. His classmate, one of the few with whom he had been reasonably close, asked him if he was interested in serving as legal counsel for a chamber of the state legislature. His classmate's offer made him realize for the first time in a long time why he had gone to law school, to engage the world in broad, creative, and helpful ways. His decision to join his classmate in legislative work was not only an easy one but also one that made his career.

The Missionary

She hadn't expected her career outcome, although in retrospect it made perfect, indeed rather incredibly rich, sense. She had been on a mission going into law school, drawing on her commitment to improve the lives of children and the poor. Her commitments were real. She had deliberately taken housing in a challenged part of her city in order to learn about and help the dignified and joyful, but struggling and scared, people whom she befriended there. She hadn't given up those commitments while in law school, either, and had instead recruited fellow students to her life- and soul-saving causes. Yet law school had shown her just how skilled she could be at learning law constructs and deploying them for good works especially in finely crafted written arguments. Her law professors and mentors noted her skill, promoting her through a series of opportunities that qualified her for select and traditional jobs that only academically superior students ordinarily qualify. When early in her third year the time came for her to give serious thought to post-graduate employment, her law professors and mentors encouraged her to apply for a research position with an appellate court, where her writing skills would have their greatest institutional value. While the position was certainly competitive, she won the job with glowing recommendation letters including from the appellate court's chief judge for whom she had interned. Her career seemed set. She might expect after a few years of this high-level judicial service to join a large firm, teach law, or do other government or corporate work. Yet a few months on the job, one with great security and good benefits, convinced her that she had missed her calling entirely. With her mentors' blessing, she resigned in favor of solo practice where she could represent children and the poor, not only advocating for their interests but also standing alongside them in the many ordinary and few extraordinary challenges that they faced. Within a few short years, her skill at writing and advocacy allowed her to add teaching, program development, and even leadership to her complex but rich professional resume. She hadn't so much found a career as *made* a career, one that fit her unique character, extraordinary skills, and powerful mission.

The Entrepreneur

He knew well before he started law school that he could be very good in building and managing a law practice. He wasn't sure yet about the law part, but from his business degrees and substantial prior management experience, he knew that he could readily handle a law practice's entrepreneurial aspects. In fact, as he made his way through law school, he discerned that he might be a whole lot better than a lot of lawyers at those strategic, management, and practice-development tasks. His third-year internship at a small firm confirmed his realization. Most lawyers seemed to have only an intuitive, habitual sense of how to make, run, and grow a law practice. For the most part, the lawyers he met and got to know didn't have his own substantial business education and experience, or his keen insight. Indeed, some of those lawyers indicated to him in one way or another that they knew, respected, and *valued* that he had marketing, systems, and other business acumen that they lacked. The business prowess that he evidenced in his internship and his coursework with various adjunct professors who practiced in the locale was already earning him job feelers. Yet as encouraging as these third-year intimations of hiring interest were, his business sense also told him that he should build a practice for himself rather than for another. So although he had clear job prospects by the time of his graduation that he only needed to pursue, he instead spent his time before and especially after the bar exam, while waiting for results, on a business plan for his own law firm. And his plan was not simply to start a solo practice. Instead, he intended to start a law firm. He scheduled his first major practice-development event for a date just after bar results would be out and, fortunately, passed the bar exam. His firm was off and running, within just a couple of years up to five lawyers, and a few more years later up to five partners. He had indeed built something valuable, both a respected law firm and sustainable business.

The Hometown

She had known her whole life that she would pursue, find, and enjoy a professional role in her hometown metropolitan area. Indeed, quite early on she had discerned that she should be a lawyer, probably a business lawyer of some kind. She chose accounting as her undergraduate program to be sure that she could handle the financial issues that she suspected good business lawyers could handle. Although she had also taken undergraduate business-law courses and still wanted to be a business lawyer, she even decided to take a few years before law school to work as an accountant to make sure she brought full value to her future business clients. During that interim, her accounting skills grew quickly to the point that she received local and even national recognition as a young professional, all of which simply confirmed for her that she should further her education with a law degree. Attending her hometown law school made perfect sense, leaving the only question where she would land a job out of law school. She did substantial investigation and research into that question early in law school. From that research, much of it online but also in networking and informational interviews, she discovered that she would probably make the best fit in a small high-reputation firm located in an upscale district, where successful and growing small businesses and local professionals might go for services. The firm would need to focus on business work, of course she knew, but should also have senior, skilled management. She knew that she needed to work with stable, responsible professionals. Once she located the handful of small firms that best fit the profile, she used her law school's career office to help her secure an internship at one of those firms. Although the firm's founding senior partner told her that they were not adding lawyers and wouldn't be making her an offer at the internship's conclusion, she nonetheless felt that her accounting experience just might make the difference. When the internship ended, no offer came at first. She busied herself finishing her last term's courses and preparing for graduation and the bar exam. But then, just a couple of weeks before the bar exam, the senior partner called with an offer. She knew that she had only needed the opportunity, and indeed, within a few short years, she was a name partner in the firm, recruiting, interviewing, evaluating, and hiring a new associate.

The Veteran

Law school had definitely been Plan B, although in retrospect, it had been a very good Plan B, the kind that made her think that maybe it had been Plan A all along. She had loved her military career, right up until she fell from the back of a large troop-transport vehicle in full combat gear. Her multiple serious internal and orthopedic injuries not only ended that career and left her facing a series of daunting back surgeries and recoveries to preserve any limited ability to ambulate but also left her with severe chronic pain. Yet somehow, her arduous path to recovery left her with a zeal to help other military members and veterans who faced similar recoveries. Indeed, her parallel path dealing with the complex career, legal, and financial implications of her military injuries, and accessing administrative programs and public and private benefits, left her with equal zeal to help other veterans and military members navigate those paths. She quickly learned that a law degree would vastly help her in doing the latter work. And so using her veterans' benefits, she earned that law degree, as soon as her injuries had healed just enough to allow her to do so. Even while in law school, she volunteered, interned, and worked in veterans' assistance programs, about which she already knew much but learned much more. She didn't plan after graduation to join a law firm, instead simply to expand her already extensive network to develop a veterans' benefits practice of her own, which she successfully did. But she also soon learned that a law firm position and office could give her greater standing in the veterans' community. By then, she knew the few firms in her locale that she would really want to join, two of which happened to have recently posted positions for hiring. After interviewing with both firms, each of which seemed quite glad to bring on a lawyer who already had a valuable niche practice, she found herself in the enviable position of having competing offers from both of them, giving her the liberty to choose the better offer, better fit, and better firm. Sometimes getting a job comes last, she thought, after first gaining a mission, then acquiring the skills to complete it, and then charging down the mission's only path.

The Confidante

She didn't fully realize it when she started law school, but she was destined to be her clients' confidante, the one professional to whom her clients' most felt that they could turn to create, preserve, or accomplish their vision. Perhaps she should have known. After earning her undergraduate accounting degree, she had spent nearly a decade helping individuals, small businesses, and corporate clients not only with accounting issues but with growth, management, service, communications, and other interests. She had come naturally to the kind of strategic thinking that her consulting on these issues required, as if she had been born to navigate changing shoals. Her accounting and law degrees simply gave her the technical knowledge and certifications to back up her natural gifts. She also carried the kind of positive energy and interest in others that tends strongly to make a professional career. As she finished her third year of law school, she was readily able to reconfirm her well-established network in the business and professional community to which she planned to return. Those contacts led to an interview at the mid-sized firm that she had most hoped to join. Impressed at her network, experience, and accounting knowledge, the firm extended her an offer that had her start right after the bar exam. She thought that she had found her career job. Yet after just a short while at the firm, barely two years, she found herself joining two partners in the firm in starting their own firm. Oddly, even though she was now a name partner in a firm led by two premier and highly experienced business lawyers, she was not really a mere junior partner. Her business acumen instead made her a key advisor in much of what the firm did in its own interests while also a key advisor in much of what the firm did for the responsible and successful individuals, small businesses, and corporate clients making up its practice core. She was a trusted advisor and confidante to the firm's clients, wise far beyond the few years of her experience as a lawyer.

The Technologist

Technology had long fascinated him, well before he even thought of going to law school. While his first undergraduate degree had been in mathematics, he had taken enough computer-science courses to easily add a second bachelor's degree in that field from another university. His undergraduate education made his information-technology services a hot commodity, as he not only wrote software and developed and administered database systems but also procured for business clients the hardware and services to support those systems. His procurement work trying to decipher the labyrinth legal agreements common in the information-technology field led his curious mind to law. When he learned that he could earn a law degree at his local law school while still working in the information-technology field, he jumped at the chance. By his third year, he was researching which local law firms served clients in structuring their information-technology purchases and agreements. He found that the largest firms tended to have larger corporate clients with in-house counsel to do their procurement legal work, while the smallest firms typically lacked the sophisticated clients who needed that work. Mid-sized firms doing small business and growth business work seemed to be his niche for information-technology work. So he targeted his networking and job applications at those firms. His discernment was accurate, and his strategy worked. A premier local mid-sized firm jumped at his application, the supporting materials for which emphasized his information-technology and procurement background. Within a short while, he was providing the law services for information-technology and procurement work for small and growing businesses throughout not only his firm's metropolitan locale but across the state. He had in a surprisingly short time not only found his niche but earned a reputation as one of the premier technology lawyers in the state.

The Timing

Timing, people say, is everything. He felt as if he had done everything right to land a job by graduation, certainly by the time that he had passed the bar exam. He had paid attention to his studies while also participating in just enough co-curricular, volunteer, and leadership activities. He had also landed an internship at a firm of two senior, high-reputation lawyers, where he had done what they said was an outstanding job with their clients' very serious matters. He was confident that he would make a good lawyer, one whom clients trusted and who would sincerely and genuinely help. Others had even told him that he had that mysterious x-factor comprised in his case of gravitas or seriousness mixed generously with optimism and leavened lightly with wry humor. Yet when his internship ended at graduation, he heard what at the time was clearly bad news that the two senior partners were unable at the moment to hire him. They explained unhelpfully that they *wanted* to hire him but that the timing, right at a lull in the firm's work freighted further by certain financial uncertainties, just wasn't right. It wasn't him or the quality of his work, they told him, but the momentary uncertainty of the firm's future, one that they were sure would soon change so that they could indeed extend an offer. He trusted that the partners were being forthright with him, although he also couldn't help wondering what he might have done differently. At that point, though, he had little choice but to proceed to the bar exam and beyond, while joining others of his fellow graduates back in the job-candidate line. What the partners had said kept resonating with him while he waited for his bar results. They wanted to hire him and were sure that they soon could. So while he made job applications at other firms, he also busied himself starting his own solo practice doing the work that he had performed so well at the firm. His solo practice grew through that first year of waiting and then into a second year when finally, he got the firm's still-welcome call. Years later, still fully enjoying his role at the firm, he was glad that he'd briefly had a solo practice to prove to himself that he had the x-factor.

The Linguist

His immigrant family had moved so far and so often when he was young that he had wondered what would become of him. How could he possibly develop a skill, identity, and career, with his family so often on the move? The strong sense of wanting to belong, with which his family's nomadic life had left him, led him to join the military. A military career, giving him that strong sense of community and identity even while he continued to travel worldwide, seemed a perfect match, and indeed, he relished the career. Already fluent in three languages, he quickly added two more in his military training so that he could serve in key intelligence roles in world hotspots. Unfortunately, one of those spots was a little too hot, leaving him with a military-career-ending combat injury. His military intelligence and administrative roles had brought him into contact with military lawyers, whose insight and advocacy skills he admired. So he went to law school drawing on his veterans' benefits, thinking that he might find a national security or similar role. Yet while in law school, he volunteered for an immigration service that reignited his immigrant affinity while drawing heavily again on his language skills. Immigration law looked like a likely career, especially after he completed an elective course in that subject and expanded his pro bono and volunteer service. Yet his military, administrative, and intelligence background seemed to serve him well in so many law fields, so much so that an adjunct professor who managed a local mid-sized law firm recruited him. He wondered again where his law career would lead. His family, who needed his financial support, made easier his decision to join the firm. That decision was when things began to come together. While the firm moved him through its practice groups so that he could meet and work with each of the firm's lawyers, he continued his pro bono immigration work. One of the firm's partners asked him to help a corporate client with an immigration matter. Then another partner asked him for similar help, and then another, each of them also drawing on his foreign-language skills. Even while he settled into one of the firm's established practice groups, he found that he was not only doing substantial immigration work but also helping other lawyers in the firm learn how to do so. In time, the firm recognized him as the chair of a new immigration practice group. He — and his career — had found a home.

The Gift

Nothing in particular had distinguished her as a likely lawyer, not academics, networks, nor communication skills, and not her family, friends, nor experience. She couldn't even articulate on her own why she had chosen law school. Maybe, she felt in retrospect, she had gone to law school because no one had thought that she either could or would. Maybe, she realized later, she became a lawyer precisely because she was an unlikely and even an ordinary lawyer. For a time, too, her law school challenges made her future look like she wasn't going to be a lawyer. Somewhere deep inside of her, though, she was absolutely determined not to give up. She also found professors who still believed that she had no clear reason to give up, that she could and would instead complete the program. Gradually, arduously, against what seemed like substantial odds, she reached the point in her third year where she could choose a clinical experience as prelude to her law career. For the first time, her choice to pursue a law career suddenly made sense. She went home to join in an internship a solo practitioner serving her rural area. There, among people whom she understood and cared about most deeply, she excelled just as surely as she had *not* excelled in law school. Her work delighted and impressed her internship supervisor, the solo practitioner, so much so that he offered to employ her as soon as she passed the bar exam. That condition, the bar exam that every lawyer faces but some find to be more of challenge than others, was her final obstacle, one that she knew that she must attack with a design, rigor, and discipline that, despite all of her hard work, she had not yet exhibited. To her great good fortune, she passed, succeeding on to a law practice that was every bit as well matched for her as her employer solo had envisioned. She was, indeed, no ordinary lawyer. While a law career seemed a gift to her, she was also clearly a very special gift to her clients.

The Switchback

His job search had looked so promising in the start but had taken one swift and unexpected turn that he had simply not expected. That turn had led to another and then another, until finally he had somehow ended up back within the promise with which his job search had begun. The twists and turns had been dizzying, like a switchback road up a mountain, but he had ended at the mountaintop. He had taken the year after law school to marry, recover from law school while leading a semblance of a normal life, and then study for and pass the bar. During that time, he had taken a low-stress job both to give a little structure to his new life while earning a little income. He had always planned, though, to enter law practice. So with bar results in hand, he updated his resume, gathered his strong recommendation letters, and working with his law school's career office applied for several posted positions in his locale, full of deserved confidence. His confidence was well placed, as it turned out, because he received offers from the first two positions for which he interviewed. His choice between the two positions was an easy one because the first of the two firms to make an offer had been his dream job. He hadn't really been interested in the other position. His only concern was with an ambiguity in the job benefits that the dream firm offered. And so he replied to the offer with a question regarding those benefits. To his surprise and disappointment, the firm's response was to rescind the offer, even though he hadn't meant to try to negotiate a better offer. He then had no choice but to take the other position. But within days of having done so, he and his new employer agreed to part ways. That job, too, hadn't worked out. Now chagrined rather than confident, he spent the next few weeks gaining another interview, fortunately one that led to an offer that he was relieved to accept, even though the job meant a difficult commute. He learned much in the next several months in that job, only to get a surprise call from the first firm, his dream firm that had made and then rescinded an offer. The firm was renewing its offer, this time with clarified and improved benefits. He gladly accepted. He had his dream job after all. His had been a dizzying ride, but he was at the mountaintop.

The Staffer

She wasn't sure when she started law school where she would end up, just sure that she would end up employed. She had good reason for her confidence. She had a foreign law degree and prior law-practice experience in another country, just not the degree and licensure that would allow her to practice in her new adopted home. As anyone might expect, her second law school program was much easier than her first, so much so that her academic standing and awards distinguished her. She had no trouble landing law-clerk work and a premier internship, and obtaining strong recommendation letters from professors and lawyers whom she helped along the way. Yet despite her academic prowess, practice experience, awards, and mentor support, she for some reason found no clear path for employment, even after taking and passing easily the state's difficult bar exam. She seemed either over qualified or under qualified for every position she sought. One firm would indicate that it preferred to train its own new lawyers through its own summer-associate program, rather than hire ready-made lawyers, while the next firm would indicate that it preferred to hire laterals who brought their own book of business. She saw classmates with lower academic ranking get offers from their law-clerk or internship sites, when she got none, while other less-experienced classmates got jobs on the open market for which she, too, had applied and that she knew she could do at least as well. The problem seemed to be that she just didn't fit any of the traditional categories well. So she took some contract work while she continued to research positions and apply, always casting her sights more and more broadly. Finally, she heard of an open position as a research attorney for an appellate court. Given her prior practice experience, she hadn't thought until then of working for a court, even though she had the top academic standing, strong research and writing skills, and awards and recommendation letters to do so. She had thought that she would find herself engaged as a practitioner in the life of her local community. Still, she realized, a job is a job, and she had a family to support. And in retrospect, her staff position with the appellate court provided her not only with the income, benefits, and security that she and her family needed but also with an undeniable professional credit that would open doors in the future, plus an immersion in her adopted home's professional culture that would improve other skills. Court staff work also relieved her of the usual practice demands, giving her extra time to devote to her immigrant family in adjusting to her adopted home. Things had worked out well after all.

The Marriage

His job search had ended up having more to do with the balance in his life and the commitment that he had made in marriage than it did with his ambition, skill, education, or opportunity. And yet, the process had somehow led him to exactly where it should have. He had taken a law clerk's job at a small local firm while in law school, working summers fulltime and then part-time throughout the school year. He had no real intention of staying at the firm, whose partners didn't expect him to stay. His classmates were interviewing for jobs all over the country, many for judicial clerkships or at large corporate firms. Indeed, he had selected his coursework and co-curricular and extra-curricular activities to qualify for those same national and corporate jobs. His wife encouraged him to interview with a premier firm at a premier location, meaning one with a booming economy, warm sunny climate, and ocean views. The firm offered him a job at triple the salary that he would have made locally, an offer that with his wife's encouragement he was glad to accept. But as the time approached for graduation, the big move, the distant state's bar exam, and the new premier job, his wife fell seriously ill. With his wife housebound and unable to move, he had no choice other than to give up the premier job with profuse apologies to the premier firm, quickly register for his home state's bar exam, and beg his small local firm to keep him on, which fortunately it did. His wife soon recovered, but by then they had learned that they were glad not to have moved to a place where they might not have handled well the fast-paced and extravagant lifestyle. He had also quickly gotten to do high-level and

141

responsible work at his small firm, and to do it so well that his income increased quickly. To make matters even better, the firm soon let him open another office in his wife's hometown while also making him a name partner. Sometimes, heeding a marriage is better for a career than chasing a career and expecting a marriage to follow.

Conclusion

A job search is like so many other seasons in life, reflective both of who you are and who you want to be. Indeed, job searching accentuates both of those things, your *I am* on the one hand and your *I want to be* on the other hand. In a job search, you must simultaneously show prospective employers who you currently are, what knowledge, skills, and aptitudes you currently possess, while also helping those employers appreciate your commitment to become a new employee with new relationships, knowledge, skills, and aptitudes, for them. That happy tension between what you have already accomplished as your resume and other job-search resources ably reflect, and what you want to accomplish for your new employer, is exactly what makes job searching so exciting and rewarding. If you can see job searching as creative and fruitful rather than as painful, stressful, or embarrassing, then you have won half the battle. You can make lemons or lemonade out of anything in life. Try making your job search something that you can value not just for the job it wins you but as the experience of a lifetime. Some professionals really only go through a meaningful job search once in a career, even if they change jobs more often. Treat your job search as your one opportunity to do something profound, which is to show the world both who you are and whom you expect to become.

Acknowledgments

As author, I thank Western Michigan University Cooley Law School and its President and Dean Don LeDuc for the mission, resources, and support to complete this book. I also thank the law school's inspired leadership team including Vice President Kathy Conklin, General Counsel James Robb, and Associate Deans Chris Church, Laura LeDuc, Amy Timmer, Joan Vestrand, Duane Strojny, Charles Mickens, Ron Sutton, and Michael McDaniel. I especially acknowledge the substantial contributions of Associate Dean for Careers & Professional Development Charles Toy whose tireless work and constant vision, and manuscript review, lent so much inspiration and insight. I also thank Grand Rapids-campus Assistant Dean Tracey Brame, Auxiliary Deans David Tarrien, Tonya Krause-Phelan, and Devin Schindler, and Professors Paul Sorensen, Victoria Vuletich, Chris Hastings, Chris Trudeau, Marjorie Gell, and Michael Molitor, for their collegial and administrative support. I also thank Head of Public Services Aletha Honsowitz and her library staff for research support, and Coordinator Danielle Hall for manuscript review, inspiration, and insight into career services. I also thank graduates Sarah Miller, Rob Howard, Holliann Willekes, Jason Van Elderen, Erin McAleer, Sharmila Rajani, Lindsay Hartmann, Mike Lichterman, Justin Wheeler, Kellen Dotson, Scott Hughes, Anna Rapa, Andy Rodenhouse, Holly Jackson, Zaneta Adams, Rachel Terpstra,

Elliott Church, Peter VanGelderen, Rob Suarez, Heather Main, Ogenna Iweajunwa, and others for their inspiration in both following the well-worn job-search path while also embracing their own unique and successful job-search experience.

About the Author

Nelson Miller is a professor and associate dean at Western Michigan University Thomas M. Cooley Law School. Before joining WMU-Cooley, Dean Miller practiced civil litigation for 16 years, representing individuals, corporations, agencies, and public and private universities. He has published over 30 books and dozens of book chapters and articles on law, law school, and law practice, and edited other books. The State Bar of Michigan recognized Dean Miller with the John W. Cummiskey Award for pro-bono service, while the law school recognized him with its Great Deeds award for similar service. He was also among about two dozen law professors recognized nationally in the Harvard University Press study *What the Best Law Teachers Do*. Dean Miller earned his law degree at the University of Michigan where he was on law review and graduated Order of the Coif, before joining the firm that later became Fajen and Miller, PLLC, his practice base before moving full-time into law teaching.

Other Law Books by Nelson Miller

Going to Law School

A Law Student's Guide

A Law Graduate's Guide

Dear J.D.: What to Do with Your Law Degree

Preparing for the Bar Exam

Lawyer Finances

Entrepreneurial Practice

Cross-Cultural Law Service

Injured – Seriously!

The Top 100 Questions Friends & Family Ask a Lawyer

The Faithful Lawyer

www.ingramcontent.com/pod-product-compliance
Lightning Source LLC
Chambersburg PA
CBHW070729220326
41598CB00024BA/3363